A Practic
Stru
Drills

A. J. Thomson
A. V. Martinet

Oxford University Press

Oxford University Press
Walton Street, Oxford OX2 6DP

Oxford New York Toronto
Delhi Bombay Calcutta Madras Karachi
Petaling Jaya Singapore Hong Kong Tokyo
Nairobi Dar es Salaam Cape Town
Melbourne Auckland

and associated companies in
Berlin Ibadan

Oxford English and the *Oxford English logo* are
trade marks of Oxford University Press

ISBN 0 19 431345 X
© Oxford University Press 1977, 1986

First published 1977
Reprinted four times
Sixth impression, reset with corrections, 1986
Ninth impression 1989

Typeset in Great Britain by
Promenade Graphics Limited, Cheltenham
Printed in Hong Kong

Contents

iv

Introduction

These drills are based on our *Practical English Grammar,* and above most of them is given the number of the relevant paragraph of the *Grammar* (fourth edition, 1986), e.g. 'PEG 104'.

Like the exercises that also accompany the *Grammar,* the drills are graded ■, ◨ and □ in order of difficulty, ■ being the most difficult. The grading is printed to the left of the references.

Recordings of the first ten items are available from the publishers, but the book can also be used where a cassette-recorder or language laboratory is not available. All the prompt sentences are printed here, and the answers are printed in the key at the end of the book.

In most of the drills the student is required to answer or make a comment on a question or statement which he or she hears from the cassette or the teacher, e.g.

A: If I sell my car . . .
B: *Oh, are you thinking of selling your car?*

But in a few of the drills the sentence the student hears is merely a prompt which must be repeated in the answer, e.g.

A: I'm not late.
B: *I'm not late, am I?*

We have aimed at making these drills as much like ordinary conversation as possible, and in most cases the vocabulary has been kept deliberately simple. We hope that teachers and students will enjoy these drills and find them useful.

A.J.T., A.V.M.

1 Auxiliary verbs: short answers

☐ PEG 108

(a) Affirmative

A: Were you here yesterday?
B: *Yes, I was.*

A: Did Ann meet Jack?
B: *Yes, she did.*

(b) Negative

A: Were you here yesterday?
B: *No, I wasn't.*

A: Did Ann meet Jack?
B: *No, she didn't.*

For convenience, treat **you** as singular, e.g.
A: Are you ready?
B: *Yes, I am.*
But **you and Tom/Ann** etc. or **you both** must of course be answered with
we, e.g.
A: Are you and Tom ready?
B: *Yes, we are.*

1 Are you both going away next weekend?
2 Did you go away last weekend?
3 Can Tom drive a car?
4 Has he got a licence?
5 Will Ann be here tomorrow?
6 Could you wait half an hour?
7 Were they late?
8 Did Bill get a lift?
9 Would he like to work abroad?
10 Must you go? (*For negative answer use* **needn't.**)
11 Is he getting on well?
12 Were they waiting for the bus?
13 Had they missed their usual bus?
14 Is he over twenty-one?
15 Does he usually go by air?
16 Have you ever fallen off a horse?
17 Was he injured in the accident?
18 Did he blame the other driver?
19 Will she be back by four?
20 Need you tell him? (*For affirmative answer use* **must.**)

2 Auxiliary verbs: short answers

☐ PEG 108

Assume that the questions are addressed to you and Tom.

(a) Affirmative and Negative

A: Can you both swim?
B: *I can but Tom can't.*

A: Were you both there?
B: *I was but Tom wasn't.*

(b) Negative and Affirmative

A: Can you both swim?
B: *I can't but Tom can.*

A: Were you both there?
B: *I wasn't but Tom was.*

1 Have you both got tickets?
2 Did you both see the play?
3 Do you both like Swedish films?
4 Are you both over twenty-one?
5 Have you both got driving licences?
6 Are you both learning to fly?
7 Will you both be here tomorrow?
8 Were you both surprised?
9 Would you both like it?
10 Must you both go? (*Use* **needn't** *for negative.*)
11 Can you both see well?
12 Do you both belong to a club?
13 Are you doing anything tonight?
14 Need you practise tonight? (*Use* **must** *in the affirmative.*)
15 Could you both work late tonight?
16 Should you have been on the plane?
17 Had you spoken to him before?
18 Would you mind if the trip was cancelled?
19 Are you both studying English?
20 Have you both got plenty of money?

3 Auxiliary verbs: negative additions to negative statements

□ PEG 112D

A: Jack couldn't understand it. (Tom)

(a) B: *Neither could Tom.*

or

(b) B: *Jack couldn't understand and neither could Tom.* (Both subjects stressed.)

A: He can't cook. (she)

(a) B: *Neither can she.*

or

(b) B: *He can't cook and neither can she.* (Both subjects stressed.)

Alternatively the same second subject could be used in all the answers, e.g.

Neither could Tom/Neither can Tom/Neither must Tom

or: *Neither could I/Neither can I* etc.

nor could be used instead of **neither**.

1 Peter hasn't time to study. (Bill)
2 George mustn't be late. (Arthur)
3 Paul didn't get any sleep. (his mother)
4 Ann doesn't smoke. (I)
5 Nancy wouldn't come. (her husband)
6 Paul doesn't believe you. (James)
7 Bill hasn't been waiting long. (Bob)
8 Andrew wasn't drunk. (Peter)
9 They don't know the way. (I)
10 Ann won't write letters. (Lucy)
11 She isn't going anywhere. (I)
12 Charles wasn't making a noise. (Jack)
13 Peter shouldn't have complained. (Paul)
14 He won't be ready by six. (she)
15 Peter hadn't done his homework. (his sister)
16 The Smiths aren't rich. (the Joneses)
17 He can't explain it. (anyone else)
18 Peter hasn't started work yet. (Harold)
19 Ann couldn't lift it. (Alice)
20 Jack hadn't been paid. (Peter)

4 Auxiliary verbs: affirmative additions to affirmative statements

☐ PEG 112A

A: Tom is going by taxi. (Bill)
B: *And so is Bill.*
or
B: *Tom is going by taxi and so is Bill.* (Both subjects stressed.)

A: She works in a laundry. (he)
B: *And so does he.*
or
B: *She works in a laundry and so does he.* (Both subjects stressed.)

Alternatively the same second subject could be used for all answers, e.g. *So is Tom/So does Tom/So will Tom* etc.
or: *So am I/So do I/So will I* etc.

1 They had cornflakes for breakfast. (I)
2 George has lunch in the canteen. (Gerald)
3 John has a hangover this morning. (Alan)
4 Jack should have thanked her. (we)
5 Ann got a parking ticket. (Alice)
6 Mary's taking photographs. (Michael)
7 She develops her own films. (he)
8 Paul thought it was too much. (I)
9 Brian should go to bed earlier. (Jane)
10 Philip will have to take lessons. (Pat)
11 They missed the programme. (we)
12 James had better change his shoes. (Mark)
13 They're looking for a flat. (we)
14 Rupert made six mistakes. (you)
15 Jack must go. (his wife)
16 Hugh liked the Albert Hall. (Mary)
17 Emily offered to help. (Jean)
18 Bill should take a holiday. (Peter)
19 Richard has just got home. (Philip)
20 I'm tired of this. (we all)

5 Auxiliary verbs: affirmative additions to negative statements

☐ PEG 112B

A: His mother didn't come to the wedding. (his father)
B: *His mother didn't come to the wedding but his father did.*
(Both subjects are normally stressed.)

1 Mary doesn't like the flat. (Tom)
2 George isn't ready. (Peter)
3 Peter wouldn't wait for you. (George)
4 Mr Jones hadn't arrived. (his wife)
5 She won't sign the protest. (her sister)
6 Bill didn't wave. (Bob)
7 Mr Jones hasn't got a driving licence. (Mrs Jones)
8 You needn't attend the meeting. (your friend) (*Use* **must.**)
9 You couldn't do it in one day. (I)
10 They weren't in any danger. (we)
11 He hadn't promised to help. (I)
12 She wouldn't like to see it. (I)
13 Ann can't read without glasses. (I)
14 They haven't got colour television. (we)
15 Bob doesn't like thrillers. (Michael)
16 The children shouldn't get up early. (their mother)
17 He hadn't noticed the mistake. (she)
18 Peter wouldn't do it for nothing. (Andrew)
19 Mary didn't buy an evening paper. (Alice)
20 The bus driver wasn't in the bus. (conductor)

6 Auxiliary verbs: negative additions to affirmative statements

☐ PEG 112C

A: George likes living alone. (Peter)
B: *George likes living alone but Peter doesn't.*

A: His brother gave him a present. (his sister)
B: *His brother gave him a present but his sister didn't.*
(Both subjects are normally stressed.)

1 Peter took the lift up. (Paul)
2 Peter had an umbrella. (Paul)
3 You were late. (I)
4 They had booked seats. (we)
5 Mary has been waiting for ages. (you)
6 She passed her driving test. (I)
7 She was taught by a qualified instructor. (I)
8 Peter can stand on his head. (his brother)
9 Mary could wear that shade of green. (I)
10 He reads the paper from cover to cover. (I)
11 They would be afraid to protest. (I)
12 The girls were amused. (the boys)
13 The girls laughed. (the boys)
14 He wears jeans. (she)
15 His hair is wavy. (hers)
16 His mother came to the prison to see him. (his father)
17 Peter has been to Japan. (his sister)
18 Bill must report to the police station. (Bob) (*Use* **needn't.**)
19 George would be horrified. (his mother)
20 Sidney believes in ghosts. (Jack)

7 Auxiliary verbs: short responses to affirmative statements

□ PEG 111

A: The train was full.
B: *Was it?*

A: I went to the cinema yesterday.
B: *Did you?*

These short responses are roughly equivalent to **really?** or **indeed?**
When said without any special intonation, they indicate a polite lack of interest. But they can also, when said with the appropriate intonation, express surprise, approval, disbelief and sometimes other emotions.

1 I go to the cinema quite often.
2 I went last night.
3 It was a very good film.
4 The queues were enormous.
5 I've finished that book you lent me.
6 I'd read it before actually.
7 I live in a very noisy street.
8 My husband thinks I'm a wonderful cook.
9 I do my best.
10 I did everything I could.
11 I must go now.
12 Diamonds suit me.
13 It's raining.
14 I like going to the opera.
15 You've made another mistake.
16 Your dog bit me again last night.
17 I'd like to go to Morocco for my holidays.
18 I have a very small appetite.
19 We've met before.
20 My garden was lovely last week.

8 Auxiliary verbs: short responses to negative statements

☐ PEG 111

A: I wasn't late.
B: *Weren't you?*

A: I didn't see him.
B: *Didn't you?*

See the note to the previous exercise.

1 I don't like your brother.
2 I couldn't sleep last night.
3 I wasn't afraid.
4 I can't type very well.
5 My wife doesn't understand me.
6 I didn't make a single mistake!
7 I haven't an enemy in the world.
8 I don't snore.
9 It can't rain like this every day.
10 I shouldn't be telling you all this.
11 I never tell lies.
12 I didn't mean to annoy you.
13 Nobody believed me! (*Use* **they** *as subject.*)
14 My case wasn't examined.
15 You aren't so clever as you think you are.
16 I wouldn't like to share a flat with you.
17 I wasn't born then.
18 They didn't treat me fairly.
19 I don't agree with you.
20 I wouldn't tell a lie even to save my life.

9 Auxiliary verbs: affirmative + interrogative responses

☐ PEG 111B

A: I borrowed your bicycle.
B: *Oh, you did, did you?* (Both verbs are stressed.)

This type of response normally indicates anger. But used without **oh** and with a rising intonation it can indicate surprise or disbelief.

1 I borrowed your car yesterday.
2 I'd like it tomorrow too.
3 You can walk to work.
4 It's good for you to walk.
5 Anyway you drive too fast.
6 You're a danger on the roads.
7 You'll have an accident one day.
8 We were talking about your driving in the pub last night.
9 Everyone agreed with me. (*Use* **they** *as subject.*)
10 I often listen in to your telephone calls.
11 They're sometimes very interesting.
12 I've taped some of the more interesting ones.
13 I told the boss you were late last Friday.
14 I always tell him when anyone is late.
15 He expects me to spy on the staff.
16 I'm being promoted next month.
17 I'd like a diamond ring for my birthday.
18 You could easily afford to buy me one.
19 You are always buying things for yourself.
20 And diamonds are quite cheap.

10 Auxiliary verbs: negative + negative interrogative responses

☐ PEG 111B

A: I don't spend anything on myself.
B: *Oh, you don't, don't you?*

A: I didn't mean to get you into trouble.
B: *Oh, you didn't, didn't you?* (Both verbs are stressed.)

This form is used in response to negative statements. It has the same meaning as its affirmative form. See the previous exercise.

1 I don't feel well enough to work today.
2 I'm not very strong.
3 I won't be able to help you tomorrow either.
4 Your letters haven't been typed yet.
5 Anyway they aren't important.
6 The typist doesn't like your handwriting.
7 And she can't always understand your sentences.
8 You don't write good English.
9 If you left this office it wouldn't make any difference.
10 You mustn't speak to me like that.
11 I'm not going to explain the new system to you.
12 Because you couldn't make it work.
13 You wouldn't even understand it.
14 Your boss doesn't think much of you.
15 He never intended to employ you.
16 But he couldn't get anyone else.
17 You shouldn't use the VIP lounge.
18 I didn't tell you the whole truth before.
19 But I wasn't really intending to deceive you.
20 You weren't really sober enough to take it in anyway.

11a Auxiliary verbs: question tags: interrogative tags after negative statements

□   PEG 110A,B

Interrogative tags after negative statements
You didn't see him, did you?

Question tags can be said with a rising intonation, as in questions, but are usually said with a falling intonation, as in statments. This intonation indicates that the speaker doesn't need information but merely expects agreement.
Use a falling intonation for this exercise.

A: I'm not late. (*prompt only*)
B: *I'm not late, am I?* (i.e. repeat the prompt and add the tag)

1   You needn't start at once.
2   His parents weren't angry.
3   You aren't doing anything tonight.
4   The tourists hadn't been inoculated.
5   Tom shouldn't have said anything.
6   Ann never reads reviews.
7   Nobody objected at the time. (*Use* **they** *in the tag.*)
8   We shan't have to wait long.
9   He hardly ever pays for his own drinks.
10   You don't expect me to wait all night.
11   This bus service isn't very reliable.
12   You couldn't drive a car down a flight of steps.
13   He wouldn't lift a finger to help anyone.
14   You won't tell Peter.
15   You can't have it both ways.

11b Auxiliary verbs: question tags: negative interrogative tags after affirmative statements

☐ PEG 110A, C

Negative interrogative tags after affirmative statements
You can go out whenever you like, can't you?

Use a falling intonation as in Exercise 11a.

A: The coffee was terrible.
B: *The coffee was terrible, wasn't it?*

1 Tom and Ann have announced their engagement.
2 They are getting married next month.
3 Bill will be disappointed.
4 He was hoping to marry her himself.
5 But he waited too long.
6 He should have proposed six months ago.
7 If he had proposed she would have accepted him.
8 But girls get tired of waiting.
9 And she had been let down by her previous boy-friend.
10 All the same it's a pity.
11 You get paid twice as much as your brother.
12 And he works much harder than you.
13 He ought to ask for more money.
14 His employers could afford to pay him more.
15 They made an enormous profit last year.

12 Auxiliary verbs: question tags

☐ PEG 110

Mixed types:
interrogative tag   You won't be late, will you?
negative interrogative tag   You'll be in time, won't you?

Use a falling intonation, as in Exercise 11.

A: You didn't have to wait long.
B: *You didn't have to wait long, did you?*

A: A bus came almost at once.
B: *A bus came almost at once, didn't it?*

1 They weren't very good jokes.
2 Nobody laughed. (*Use* **they**.)
3 There must have been some mistake.
4 It's no use crying over spilt milk.
5 You will be careful.
6 They hadn't met before.
7 Everyone should be paid the same. (*Use* **they**.)
8 Then there wouldn't be any more wage claims.
9 I'm in time.
10 We'd better hurry.
11 You didn't expect him to get the job.
12 He was quite astonished himself.
13 But it'll mean living in London.
14 He won't like that.
15 He'd much rather go on living here.
16 You can manage on your own.
17 You don't want me to help you.
18 Anyway I'm not much use.
19 You aren't listening to the radio.
20 So we might as well turn it off.

13 Auxiliary verbs: question tags with a rising intonation

☐ PEG 110D

Question tags are said with a rising intonation when the speaker is not quite sure that the statement is true and wants to be re-assured. The statement here carries a fairly strong stress. The position of the stress will, of course, vary according to the speaker's meaning, so most of the following sentences could be stressed in a number of ways. But when doing the drill you should copy the stress pattern of the prompt. Notice that there is normally a rise of pitch on the stressed words.

A: You like Peter.

B: *You like Peter, don't you?*

A: They didn't take your passport.

B: *They didn't take your passport, did they?*

1 Paul caught the 8.40.
2 Ann hasn't been paid yet.
3 The snow will be too soft to ski on.
4 They could get a loan.
5 You don't think it was my fault.
6 The detectives won't search this house.
7 That bottle was full this morning.
8 He usedn't to drink so much.
9 You aren't going to do anything stupid.
10 He wouldn't leave the country without telling us.
11 You meant what you said last night.
12 We'd better call the Fire Brigade.
13 The snakes aren't dangerous.
14 Good steak can be eaten raw.
15 We aren't being followed.
16 No one suspects us. (*Use* **they**.)
17 The doctors warned you about the side-effects of the drug.
18 The water should have been boiled.
19 The fine needn't be paid at once.
20 You'd rather drive than be driven.

14 Auxiliary verbs: can and can't

□

This is a pronunciation and stress exercise. can here is unstressed and pronounced /kən/ (/kæn/ is also possible, but practise the /kən/ sound here). can't always carries a certain stress to distinguish it from can. Note also that the 'a' in can is quite different from the 'a' in can't. can't is pronounced /kɑ:nt/. Answer the questions, using /kən/ and /kɑ:nt/.

A: Can you swim and dive?
B: *I can swim but I can't dive.*

1 Can you knit and sew?
2 Can the baby walk and run?
3 Can she act and sing?
4 Can he read and write?
5 Can you draw and paint?
6 Can you ski and skate?
7 Can you type and take shorthand?
8 Can you drive and read a map?
9 Can you milk a cow and make butter?
10 Can you trot and gallop?
11 Can you change a wheel and mend a puncture?
12 Can you wash and iron?
13 Can you row and sail a boat?
14 Can you keep accounts and do income tax returns?
15 Can you light a fire and put up a tent?
16 Can you understand and speak English?
17 Can you take a temperature and give injections?
18 Can you make biscuits and cakes?
19 Can you play cards and do card tricks?
20 Can you stand on your head and walk on your hands?

15 Auxiliary verbs: **have** + object + past participle

☑ PEG 119

A: Do you clean windows yourself?
B: *No. I have them cleaned.*

A variety of tenses will be used.

1 Did you paint the house yourself?
2 Do you cut the grass yourself?
3 Are you going to mend the puncture yourself?
4 Does he wash his car himself?
5 Does she polish the floors herself?
6 Are you going to shorten the trousers yourself?
7 Do you type the reports yourself?
8 Would you adjust your brakes yourself?
9 Are you dyeing the curtains yourself?
10 Did you tow the car yourself?
11 Are you going to cut down the tree yourself?
12 Did you repair the clock yourself?
13 Do you sharpen the knives yourself?
14 Does he tune his piano himself?
15 Does she sweep the stairs herself?
16 Is he teaching his children to ride himself?
17 Did he build the new garage himself?
18 Did he plant the trees himself?
19 Is she translating the book herself?
20 Is she making the wedding cake herself?

16 Auxiliary verbs: **have** + object + past participle

☑ PEG 119

A: Did she have the window repaired? (*stress on* **have**)
B: *No, she repaired it herself.*

A: Did they have the central heating put in? (*stress on* **have**)
B: *No, they put it in themselves.*

Remember that in **myself, themselves** etc. the last syllable is stressed.

1 Did she have the coat shortened?
2 Does she have her carpets cleaned?
3 Is he going to have the car re-sprayed?
4 Does the manager have the accounts checked?
5 Did you have the ceiling whitewashed?
6 Did he have his will drawn up?
7 Did you have a television aerial put up?
8 Does he have his boots mended?
9 Are you having the trees planted?
10 Are you going to have the grapes picked?
11 Does she have her stairs swept?
12 Does she have the children taken to school every day?
13 Do you have your gutters cleaned?
14 Did you have the tyre pressures checked?
15 Does she have her hair set?
16 Did he have the leaflets delivered?
17 Does she have the pictures framed?
18 Is he having the film developed?
19 Did he have the tree cut down?
20 Did he have his tooth taken out?

17 Auxiliary verbs: **had to**

☑ PEG 144, 145F

Prompt: I missed the last bus.
B: *I missed the last bus and (I) had to walk home.*
or
B: *I missed the last bus, so I had to walk home.*

Any logical answer is acceptable, provided **had to** is used.

Prompts:

1 I missed the first bus.
2 There were no seats on the train.
3 There were no porters at the station.
4 I hadn't any change for the ticket machine.
5 I lost my dictionary.
6 I couldn't find a hotel.
7 We didn't know the way.
8 I had no cash on me.
9 I had forgotten his number.
10 When I got to the door I found that I had lost my key.
11 My phone wasn't working.
12 Our lift was out of order.
13 He had a puncture.
14 The lights went out during dinner.
15 I didn't understand the document.
16 My licence was out of date.
17 We couldn't eat the hostel meals.
18 She couldn't hear what he was saying.
19 One of the engines failed just after take-off.
20 I couldn't put the fire out myself.

18 Auxiliary verbs: **didn't have to**

☑ PEG 149

A (an old man): When I was at school we called the masters 'Sir'. It was compulsory.

B (a young man who was at the same school): *Oh, we didn't have to call the masters 'Sir'*.

When I was at school we . . . It was compulsory.

1 wore suits
2 talked French at meals
3 got up at six
4 washed in cold water
5 ran round the playground before breakfast
6 were in bed by ten
7 learnt a Shakespeare play by heart
8 cleaned our own rooms
9 made our own beds
10 looked after our own clothes
11 kept our hair short
12 served ourselves at meals
13 ate everything on our plates
14 helped with the washing up
15 worked on Saturday
16 wrote home every week
17 let the staff see our letters
18 asked permission to go into the town
19 did military training
20 played football

19 Auxiliary verbs: **had better** + infinitive without **to**

☑ PEG 120

A: I haven't told Tom yet.
B: *Then you'd better tell him today.* (**had** here is normally contracted.)

I haven't . . . yet

1 done the ironing
2 apologized
3 explained
4 applied
5 enrolled
6 finished my essay
7 washed the car
8 mended the fuse
9 fixed the aerial
10 paid the rent
11 returned the books
12 decided
13 suggested it
14 booked the seats
15 ordered the coal
16 advertised the house
17 answered his letter
18 reported the accident
19 renewed my licence
20 seen Tom about it

20 Auxiliary verbs: **be** + infinitive

■   PEG 114A

It is evening and a group of people engaged in a team activity have been given their instructions for the next day. Martin wants to know what the others have been told to do. They always use Jack's name in their reply.

A: You went with John today, didn't you?
B: *Yes, but I'm to go with Jack tomorrow.*

A: Bill carried John's equipment today, didn't he?
B: *Yes, but he's to carry Jack's equipment tomorrow.*

 1   Ann looked after Peter's children today, didn't she?
 2   Peter and Mary worked with Tom's group today, didn't they?
 3   You followed Bill today, didn't you?
 4   You drove Bill's car today, didn't you?
 5   Mary led Tom's team today, didn't she?
 6   George rode Peter's horse today, didn't he?
 7   You relieved Bill today, didn't you?
 8   You acted as lookout for Tom today, didn't you?
 9   They took their orders from Bill today, didn't they?
10   You trained with Peter today, didn't you?
11   You stood in front of Bill today, didn't you?
12   They tested Peter today, didn't they?
13   Mary filmed Andrew's group today, didn't she?
14   You navigated for Peter today, didn't you?
15   You and Hugo gave Charles a lift, didn't you?

21 Auxiliary verbs: **be** + infinitive

☑ PEG 114A

A: What were your instructions about phoning Bill?
B: *I was to phone him at 6.00.*

(This exercise could also be practised with other persons: e.g. What were his/her/your (plural) /their/my instructions?)

What were your instructions about . . .

1 reporting?
2 posting the documents?
3 meeting George?
4 contacting Ann?
5 seeing the agents?
6 collecting the film?
7 relieving Andrew?
8 joining?
9 leaving?
10 paying the workmen?
11 releasing the prisoners?
12 inspecting the camp?
13 taking off?
14 starting?
15 opening the doors?

22 Auxiliary verbs: be + perfect infinitive

■ PEG 114A

A: Did you borrow a car?
B: *No. We were to have borrowed a car but the plan fell through.*

Keep the nouns unchanged.

Did you . . .

1 camp on the beach?
2 hire a boat?
3 visit the island?
4 anchor in the bay?
5 explore the caves?
6 bathe by moonlight?
7 spend a week there?
8 collect driftwood?
9 cook over open fires?
10 make a film of the seabirds?
11 swim before breakfast?
12 water-ski?
13 keep a temperature chart?
14 get up at dawn?
15 record the dawn chorus?
16 climb the cliffs?
17 search for the sunken treasure-ship?
18 take photographs under water?
19 have sing-songs round the camp fire?
20 invite everyone to a barbecue?

23 Auxiliary verbs: **may/might** + perfect infinitive

■ PEG 113

The speakers are wondering what happened to certain things/people.

A: Perhaps she took it with her.

B: *Well, she may have taken it away with her, I suppose.* (**might** could also be used.)

A: What did you say?

B: *I said she might have taken it with her.* (*Omit* **suppose.**)

Perhaps . . .

1 he stole it.
2 she sold it.
3 you lost it. (*Use* 'I' *in the answer.*)
4 she drank it.
5 he threw it away.
6 they pawned it.
7 she left it at home.
8 he ate it.
9 they hid it in the attic.
10 he burnt it.
11 she tore it up.
12 she forgot to claim it.
13 they had an accident.
14 their car broke down. (*Use* **it** *as subject.*)
15 he advised them not to come.
16 he fell overboard.
17 they got lost.
18 he was murdered.
19 something delayed them. (*Keep* **something.**)
20 he took the wrong drug.

24 Auxiliary verbs: **may/might be working** and **may/might have been working**

☑ PEG 132B

(a) A: Perhaps he is working for Jones.
B: *Yes, he may be working for Jones.*

(b) A: Perhaps he was working for Jones.
B: *Yes, he may have been working for Jones.*

Both exercises can also be done with **might** instead of **may**.

(a) *Perhaps* . . .

1 he is waiting for someone.
2 they are wondering what to do.
3 she is trying to confuse us.
4 they are window-shopping.
5 she is expecting a letter from us.
6 he is blackmailing her.
7 they are working overtime.
8 he is looking for another job.
9 he is listening at the keyhole.
10 they are watching television.
11 he is following us.
12 he is learning karate.
13 she is telling his fortune.
14 he is showing her the way.
15 she is doing exercises.
16 they are burying something.
17 she is bird-watching.
18 she is comparing prices.
19 he is taking drugs.
20 they are helping the police.

(b) *Perhaps* . . .

1 he was waiting for someone.
2 they were wondering what to do.

i.e. just as in (a), but replacing **is/are** by **was/were**

25 Auxiliary verbs: **should have done** etc.

☑ PEG 143

A: I told him a week later.
B: *You should have told him at once.* (**should have** is normally
shortened to **should've** in speech.)

1 I asked him a week later.
2 I paid the bill a week later.
3 I thanked him a week later.
4 I looked for it a week later.
5 I invited him a week later.
6 I apologized a week later.
7 I sent it back a week later.
8 I returned a week later.
9 I reported the break-in a week later.
10 I booked the tickets a week later.
11 I answered his letter a week later.
12 I cooked it a week later.
13 I wrote to him a week later.
14 I rang him a week later.
15 I started a week later.
16 I began a week later.
17 I ate it a week later.
18 I spoke to him a week later.
19 I gave it to him a week later.
20 I complained a week later.

26 Auxiliary verbs: **shouldn't have done** etc.

☑ PEG 143

A: I only told Peter. (*stress on* **Peter**)
B: *You shouldn't have told anyone.* (**have** should be shortened to 've in speech; **any** is stressed.)

1 I only asked Mike.
2 I only invited Jack.
3 I only reported George.
4 I only paid Mary.
5 I only fined Brian.
6 I only sacked Andrew.
7 I only complained about Mark.
8 I only argued with Tom.
9 I only played with Mary.
10 I only discussed it with Alec.
11 I only talked about it with Arthur.
12 I only woke Margaret.
13 I only wrote to Bill.
14 I only shouted at Alice.
15 I only threw stones at Martin.
16 I only told lies to John.
17 I only robbed Peter.
18 I only cheated Alec.
19 I only winked at Oliver.
20 I only kissed James.

27 Auxiliary verbs: **Should I?** + perfect infinitive

■ PEG 143

(i) A: You didn't follow Bill?
   B: *No. Should I have followed him?*

(ii) A: You didn't take off your shoes?
   B: *No. Should I have taken them off?* (Notice the word order.)

You didn't . . .

1 read the instructions?
2 try to stop her?
3 listen to their conversation?
4 tip the waiter?
5 follow them?
6 keep the receipt?
7 threaten him?
8 stand up?
9 refuse?
10 offer to help?
11 make her wear her life-jacket?
12 put up the notice? (*See* (ii) *above.*)
13 take down the old programme? (*See* (ii) *above.*)
14 wear your dark glasses?
15 bring your parachute?
16 notify the authorities?
17 lock up the tapes? (*See* (ii) *above.*)
18 burn the documents?
19 give back his passport? (*See* (ii) *above.*)
20 ring the alarm bell?

28 Auxiliary verbs: shouldn't be doing and should have done

■ PEG 142, 143

A: Look at that man shaving while he drives!
B: *He shouldn't be shaving now. He should have shaved before he left the house.*

1 Look at that woman doing her nails in the bus queue!
2 Look at that man correcting exercises in the bus!
3 Look at that man polishing his shoes in the bus shelter!
4 Look at that boy tying his shoelaces as he goes into school!
5 Look at that woman putting on her earrings on the stairs!
6 Look at that girl sewing on a button in the library!
7 Look at that man eating his breakfast as he walks down the path!
8 Look at that girl putting on her make-up in the bus queue!
9 Look at that man brushing his coat in the lift!
10 Look at that man putting in his contact lenses on the escalator!
11 Look at that man filing his nails in the bar!
12 Look at that boy combing his hair in the classroom!
13 Look at that women cleaning her glasses while she drives!
14 Look at those children doing their homework in the bus!
15 Look at that man putting in his false teeth in the street!

29 Auxiliary verbs: **should/shouldn't** + continuous infinitive, present and perfect

■ PEG 142, 143

Ann, a student at a summer school, has the following programme:

7.00 – 7.30	get dressed	2.00 – 2.30 rest
7.30 – 8.00	(have) breakfast	2.30 – 3.30 work in garden
8.00 – 8.30	wash up	3.30 – 4.30 (play) tennis
8.30 – 9.30	(do) PT	4.30 – 5.00 tea
9.30 – 10.00	watch television programme	5.00 – 6.00 practise the piano
		6.00 – 7.00 rehearse play
10.00 – 10.30	discuss programme	7.00 – 7.30 supper
		7.20 – 8.00 type lecture notes
10.30 – 12.00	(attend) lectures	8.00 – 9.00 read in library
12.00 – 1.00	help with lunch	11.30 lights out
1.00 – 2.00	(have) lunch	

(a) A: It's 7.20 and Ann is sleeping.
B: *She shouldn't be sleeping. She should be getting dressed.*

(b) A: At 7.20 yesterday Ann was sleeping.
B: *She shouldn't have been sleeping. She should have been getting dressed.*

(a) *It's . . . and Ann is . . .*   (b) *At . . . Ann was . . .*

1	7.45 . . . getting up	e.g.
2	8.15 . . . having breakfast	1 At 7.45 Ann was getting up.
3	8.45 . . . washing up	i.e. as in (a) but replacing *is* by
4	9.45 . . . doing PT	**was**
5	10.15 . . . watching television	
6	12.30 . . . listening to a lecture	
7	2.15 . . . playing tennis	
8	2.45 . . . resting	
9	3.45 . . . working in the garden	
10	5.15 . . . having tea	
11	6.15 . . . practising the piano	
12	7.15 . . . rehearsing the play	
13	7.45 . . . having supper	
14	8.15 . . . typing her lecture notes	
15	12.00 . . . listening to records	

30

30 Auxiliary verbs: **must have done** (deduction)

☑ PEG 158

Martin and Simon have just come back to their house after a weekend.
Martin notices various changes; Simon thinks these must be the result
of actions by Peter, who shares the house with them.

(i) A: The door's open! (leave)
    B: *Peter must have left it open.*

(ii) A: The library books have disappeared. (take back to the library)
    B: *Peter must have taken them back to the library.* (Notice the word
       order.)

1 My torch isn't here! (borrow)
2 The plates are all clean! (wash up)
3 What are all these books doing here? (leave)
4 The teapot is in pieces! (drop)
5 How shiny the furniture looks! (polish)
6 The steps are unusually clean! (sweep)
7 There are some sandwiches on the kitchen table! (make)
8 I've turned the key but the door won't open! (bolt)
9 Here's the receipted bill! (pay)
10 There's a man at the door with a crate of beer! (order)
11 There are no biscuits left! (eat)
12 And there's no whisky left! (drink)
13 There are two policemen at the door asking about our break-in!
   (report)
14 The place is full of empty bottles! (have a party)
15 The car is in a terrible state! (drive into a wall)
16 The clock is going again! (wind)
17 There's blood all over the kitchen floor! (cut himself)
18 The bath's overflowing! (leave the tap on)
19 Where have the curtains gone to? (take down) (*See* (ii) *above.*)
20 There's a new poster on the wall! (put up) (*See* (ii) *above.*)

31 Auxiliary verbs: **couldn't** + perfect infinitive (negative deduction)

■ PEG 159

Yesterday someone finished the wine/broke a wineglass/borrowed Mary's radio etc. Mary thinks it was Tom who did these things, but you know that Tom was out all day.

A: I wonder who broke the glass. I expect it was Tom.
B: *Tom couldn't have broken it. He wasn't here yesterday.*

I wonder who . . . I expect it was Tom.

1 spoke to her
2 paid the milkman
3 brought the flowers
4 fixed the television set
5 tuned my guitar
6 made all this mess
7 moved the piano
8 spilt the wine
9 opened my letters
10 borrowed my umbrella
11 answered the phone
12 finished the bottle of gin
13 drank all the beer
14 ate the cold meat
15 fused the lights
16 left the gas on
17 let the cats out
18 overheard us
19 planted the rose bushes
20 went off with the telephone directory

32 Auxiliary verbs: **couldn't have done**

■ PEG 159

A: He says he saw Mary at the dance. (But B knows that Mary wasn't there.)

B: *He couldn't have seen her. She wasn't there.*

A: He says he escaped through the window. (But B knows that the window is barred.)

B: *He couldn't have escaped through the window. It's barred.*

The information known to B will be placed in brackets after A's statement. The words 'But B knows that . . . ' will be omitted.

He says he . . .

1 had an argument with Tom at the party. (Tom wasn't there.)
2 bolted the door. (It has no bolt.)
3 used the Emergency Exit. (There isn't one.)
4 came up by the lift. (The lift wasn't working.)
5 slept in room 13. (There is no room 13.)
6 bought it in Harrods on Sunday. (Harrods doesn't open on Sunday.)
7 hired a sailing boat in St. James's Park. (There are no boats for hire in St. James's Park.)
8 drove across Hungerford Bridge. (It is for trains and pedestrians only.)
9 took the Piccadilly Line to High Street Kensington. (The Piccadilly Line doesn't pass through High Street Kensington.)
10 carried it himself. (It weighs a ton.)
11 dined in a restaurant on top of Nelson's Column. (There is no restaurant there.)
12 waded across the Thames at Westminster Bridge. (It is too deep.)
13 watched Westminster Bridge lifting up to let a ship through. (This bridge doesn't lift up.)
14 saw the Queen standing in a queue. (The Queen doesn't stand in queues.)
15 was attacked by wolves when crossing Hampstead Heath. (There are no wolves there.)
16 walked from Chelsea to Kew in half an hour. (It is too far.)
17 got sunburnt in Hyde Park in November. (The sun isn't strong enough.)
18 swam across the Irish Sea. (It is too wide.)
19 heard your clock strike. (My clock doesn't strike.)
20 went there by train. (The railway line is closed.)

33 Auxiliary verbs: **needn't have done/could have done**

■ PEG 154

A: You sent the sheets to the laundry, I suppose? (wash them myself)
B: *No, I washed them myself.*
C: *You needn't have washed them yourself. You could have sent them to the laundry.*

1 You went by taxi, I suppose? (take a bus)
2 You went by bus, I suppose? (walk)
3 You took the lift, I suppose? (walk up the stairs)
4 You phoned him, I suppose? (write)
5 You got the tube tickets from a machine, I suppose? (stand in a queue)
6 You borrowed the books, I suppose? (buy)
7 You asked the shop to send the parcels home, I suppose? (carry them)
8 You painted the car yourself, I suppose? (have it sprayed)
9 You sewed it by hand, I suppose? (use the machine)
10 You walked up the ski-slope, I suppose? (take the ski-lift)
11 You paid by cheque, I suppose? (pay by cash)
12 You dialled the Paris number direct, I suppose? (ask the exchange to get)
13 You replaced the bulb yourself, I suppose? (send for the electrician)
14 When the curtain caught fire you put it out yourself, I suppose? (ring for the Fire Brigade)
15 You covered the grand piano with a sheet before you painted the ceiling, I suppose? (moved it out of the room)
16 A button fell off your coat so you sewed it on, I suppose? (throw the coat away)
17 You went second class, I suppose? (go first class)
18 A fuse blew so you put in a new fuse, I suppose? (sit in the dark)
19 You left your heavy case at the station, I suppose? (take it with me)
20 As you needed a copy you used a carbon, I suppose? (type it twice)

34 Auxiliary verbs: **needn't have done/could have done**

■ PEG 154

A: I had my television set repaired. It was very expensive.
B: *But you needn't have had it repaired; you could have repaired it*
   yourself.

Stress **had** and **yourself.**

have in **needn't have** and **could have** should be pronounced as if
written **'ve.**

This exercise could also be done with **shouldn't have** and **should have** or
oughtn't to have and **ought to have.**

I had . . . It was very expensive.

1   the house painted.
2   the curtains dyed.
3   the carpet cleaned.
4   the dead tree cut down. (*Note order with pronoun object: cut* it *down.*)
5   double-glazing put in. (*Note order with pronoun object: put* it *in.*)
6   central heating installed.
7   my refrigerator repaired.
8   my roof mended.
9   the roses pruned.
10 the windows washed.
11 the car resprayed.
12 the hall repapered.
13 fruit trees planted.
14 the garage built.
15 the new path made.
16 the picture framed.
17 the car polished.
18 the new lock fitted.
19 the apples picked.
20 the piano tuned.

35 Auxiliary verbs: **Couldn't you have done?** or **Shouldn't you have done?**

■ PEG 154

A: I got there on Tuesday.
B: *Couldn't you have got there before?* (= Wouldn't this have been possible?)

1 I posted it on Tuesday.
2 They paid me on Tuesday.
3 She started on Tuesday.
4 He brought it back on Tuesday.
5 He sent in his application on Tuesday.
6 I phoned him on Tuesday.
7 They moved out on Tuesday.
8 We left on Tuesday.
9 She wrote on Tuesday.
10 He applied on Tuesday.
11 He booked the tickets on Tuesday.
12 They reported it to the police station on Tuesday.
13 We re-addressed the letters on Tuesday.
14 I got back on Tuesday.
15 I made the arrangements on Tuesday.
16 I cancelled the tickets on Tuesday.
17 I answered his letter on Tuesday.
18 I gave her the message on Tuesday.
19 We invited him on Tuesday.
20 I told them about it on Tuesday.

Alternatively the exercise could be done with **should**.

A: I got there on Tuesday.
B: *Shouldn't you have got there before?* (=Don't you think it was your duty to get there before?)

36

36 Tenses: simple present

☐ PEG 173

A: Do you mend his socks?
B: *No, he mends his own socks.*

Do you . . .

1 iron his shirts?
2 wash his sheets?
3 make her bed?
4 tie his tie (for him)?
5 brush his hair?
6 choose his clothes?
7 sew on his buttons?
8 clean his shoes?
9 get his breakfast?
10 do her shopping?
11 cook his meals?
12 polish her furniture?
13 check his brakes?
14 pump up his tyres?
15 do his washing up?
16 clean his flat for him?
17 cut her hair?
18 get his tickets for him?
19 type his letters?
20 pay his bills?

37 Tenses: simple present

☐ PEG 173

A: I get up early.
B: *Tom gets up early too.*

1 I work in London.
2 I live in Hampstead.
3 I get up early.
4 I go for a walk before breakfast.
5 I have a cold bath every morning.
6 I run all the way to the station.
7 I come to work by tube.
8 I usually catch the 8.20 train.
9 I usually get a ticket from the machine.
10 I read the paper in the train.
11 I get out at Piccadilly.
12 I start work at 9.00.
13 I lunch in the canteen.
14 I finish work at 5.30.
15 I go home by bus.
16 I stand in a long queue every night.
17 I sit upstairs.
18 I buy an evening paper.
19 I arrive home about 6.30.
20 I say, 'Hello!'

38 Tenses: simple present

☑ PEG 173

A: What do you have for breakfast? Bacon and eggs?
B: *Yes, I have bacon and eggs. What do you have?* (stress on **you**)

1 Where do you eat? In the canteen?
2 What time do you start? Nine?
3 What time do you finish? Six?
4 How much do you weigh? Ten stone?
5 How tall are you? Six foot?
6 What time do you get up? Seven?
7 What animal do you like best? Dogs?
8 How do you come to the office? By bus?
9 What do you do in the evening? Watch television?
10 Where do you go for your holidays? Scotland?
11 How many weeks' holiday do you have? Three?
12 Where do you keep your money? Under the mattress?
13 Where do you buy your clothes? Paris?
14 When do you do your homework? Just before the lesson?
15 How often do you write home? Every week?
16 How do you like your coffee? Strong?
17 What do you cook on? Gas?
18 What game do you play best? Tennis?
19 Where do you swim? In the swimming baths?
20 What do you drink? Gin?

39 Tenses: simple present

☑ PEG 173

A: I read The Times.	A: I grind my own coffee.
B: *Tom reads the Express.*	B: *Tom buys his ready ground.*
A: I go out every evening.	A: I wash my own sheets.
B: *Tom stays at home.*	B: *Tom sends his to the laundry.*

i.e. Any answer is acceptable provided it begins with a 3rd person singular subject + verb in the simple present tense (affirmative), and contrasts with A's statement.

1 I smoke cigars.
2 I live on the top floor.
3 I spend very little.
4 I walk to work.
5 I work on Saturdays.
6 I usually travel by air.
7 I write with my left hand.
8 I eat with chopsticks.
9 I drink wine with my meals.
10 I watch football on television.
11 I usually go away for weekends.
12 I do my own electrical repairs.
13 I sleep with the windows open.
14 I dictate my letters to a secretary.
15 I write my essays in ordinary handwriting.
16 I speak English at meals.
17 I disagree with him.
18 I think an electric typewriter is an unnecessary luxury.
19 I wear my hair short.
20 I make a lot of mistakes.

40 Tenses: simple present

☐ PEG 173

A: I earn £50 a week.
B: *How much does your brother earn?* (stress on **brother**)

A: I live in Westminster.
B: *Where does your brother live?* (stress on **brother**)

Make questions using **how, where, when, how much, how many, how often, what.**

1 I live in Tunbridge Wells.
2 I smoke twenty cigarettes a day.
3 I have toast and coffee for breakfast.
4 I read detective stories.
5 I go to York for my holidays.
6 I spend £2 a week on fares.
7 I drive a Mini.
8 I wear rubber boots.
9 I employ twenty men.
10 I bank at Barclays.
11 I pay by cheque.
12 I like comedies best.
13 I clean my flat at weekends. (*Use* **his** *for* **my**, *and stress it slightly.*)
14 I keep my bicycle in the hall. (*See above.*)
15 I sing folk-songs.
16 I play the bagpipes.
17 I phone home every week.
18 I always sit at the back of the class.
19 I collect coins.
20 I write sentimental novels.

41 Tenses: simple present, negative

☐ PEG 173

A: Tom's making a lot of mistakes!
B: *He doesn't usually make mistakes.* (stress on **usually**)

1 Tom's answering the telephone!
2 He's taking the children to school!
3 He's helping his wife!
4 He's looking after the baby!
5 He's walking the dog!
6 He's carrying his wife's basket!
7 He's cleaning the windows!
8 He's mowing the lawn!
9 He's weeding the garden!
10 He's hanging out the washing!
11 They're spending their holidays at home!
12 I'm doing a crossword puzzle! (*Use* **puzzles** in answer.)
13 They're working late!
14 I'm knocking off early!
15 She's cooking it in butter!
16 She's baking bread!
17 He's looking miserable!
18 The dog is sleeping on your bed!
19 She's driving her husband's car!
20 She's stopping at the traffic lights!

42 Tenses: two present tenses, interrogative negative

■ PEG 166, 173

A: John spends the winters in the Bahamas.
B: *Doesn't his sister spend the winters in the Bahamas as well?*

A: John's going on a cruise this spring?
B: *Isn't his sister going on a cruise this spring as well?*

Note that some sentences are in the present continuous tense, some are in the simple present tense.

1 John goes skiing at Christmas.
2 John drives an Alfa Romeo.
3 John lives in a penthouse in Park Lane.
4 John is learning to fly a helicopter.
5 John loses a lot of money gambling.
6 John is planning to buy a Greek island.
7 John drinks champagne for breakfast.
8 John gives marvellous parties.
9 John knows a lot of important people.
10 John plays polo.
11 John employs a private bodyguard.
12 John is building a second swimming pool.
13 John is buying an enormous yacht.
14 John collects Old Masters.
15 John is starting a private zoo.
16 John spends a fortnight in a health resort every year.
17 John eats off gold plates.
18 John is terrified of being kidnapped.
19 John is always grumbling about high taxation.
20 John is thinking of moving to a tax-haven.

43 Tenses: two present tenses

☐ PEG 166, 173

A: He usually smokes Turkish cigarettes.
B: *But today he is smoking French cigarettes.*

A: He usually reads a German paper.
B: *But today he is reading a French paper.*

Do the following exercises in the same way, always substituting **French** for the adjective of nationality or the language mentioned.

He usually . . .

1 drives a German car.
2 rides an English horse.
3 sings German songs.
4 plays Italian music.
5 drinks English beer.
6 dances with a Greek girl.
7 uses an English dictionary.
8 has lunch in a Japanese restaurant.
9 listens to the news in English.
10 writes in Spanish.
11 goes to Indian films. (*Use* **a French film** *in the answer.*)
12 talks English.
13 corrects the Spanish essays.
14 explains in English.
15 lectures in Spanish.
16 broadcasts in Spanish.
17 addresses students in English.
18 cooks a Spanish meal for us.
19 travels by an Italian airline.
20 swears in Italian.

44 Tenses: two present tenses

☑ PEG 166, 173

A (in tones of great astonishment): Tom is drinking beer!
B: *Doesn't he usually drink beer?* (stress on **usually**)

1 Peter is going second class!
2 Ann is smoking a cigar!
3 Mary is doing football pools!
4 Mrs Smith is wearing a wig!
5 George is washing up!
6 Andrew is buying roses for his wife!
7 Paul is telling lies!
8 The boss is having lunch in the canteen!
9 Andrew is cooking the breakfast!
10 Peter is making his bed!
11 Mr Jones is typing his own letters.
12 The boss is standing in a queue.
13 Tom is sitting beside Margaret!
14 Bill is dancing with Alice!
15 Mrs Jones is playing roulette!
16 George is listening to our conversation!
17 Sara is going abroad for her holiday!
18 His business is making a profit!
19 Peter is going on strike with the others!
20 He is getting Christmas Day off!

45 Tenses: two present tenses

☑ PEG 166, 173

A: The staff don't usually wear sandals in the office.
B: *Then why are they wearing sandals today?*

1 Mr Jones doesn't usually grumble.
2 The canteen staff don't usually complain.
3 The boss doesn't usually swear.
4 They don't usually pay us in dollars.
5 He doesn't usually write with his left hand.
6 They don't usually walk to work.
7 He doesn't usually lunch alone.
8 She doesn't usually stand by the window.
9 He doesn't usually sit with his feet on the desk.
10 The boss doesn't usually use a calculator.
11 She doesn't usually criticize us.
12 He doesn't usually make a fuss about nothing.
13 She doesn't usually bring the tea round.
14 The boss doesn't usually smile at us.
15 They don't usually leave early.
16 He doesn't usually lock the filing cabinets.
17 He doesn't usually type his own letters. (*Omit* **own.**)
18 He doesn't usually empty the wastepaper baskets himself. (*Omit* **himself.**)
19 He doesn't usually take papers home.
20 He doesn't usually watch the clock.

46 Tenses: present and past continuous

◪ PEG 171A, 308B

A: If I go by bus—
B (interrupting): *Oh, are you thinking of going by bus?*
A: What did you say?
B: *I asked if you were thinking of going by bus.*

A: If I ring Peter—
B (interrupting): *Oh, are you thinking of ringing Peter?*
A: What did you say?
B: *I asked if you were thinking of ringing Peter.*

If I . . .

1 sell the car—
2 leave tomorrow—
3 give up my job—
4 ask Jack—
5 emigrate to Australia—
6 buy a dog—
7 hire a car—
8 sleep in a tent—
9 go to Morocco—
10 send a telegram—
11 have him followed—
12 complain to the manager—
13 threaten him—
14 offer him a bribe—
15 rob a bank—
16 paint the house myself—
17 hitch-hike—
18 report it to the police—
19 apply for the job—
20 throw a brick through his window—

47 Tenses: present and past continuous

■ PEG 166, 179

A: John's reading The Times.
B: *No, he isn't. He's reading the Telegraph.*

A: Tom was waiting for a bus.
B: *No, he wasn't. He was waiting for a taxi.*

The student must disagree with the first remark and repeat it with another suitable noun.

Remember that the first auxiliary **isn't, wasn't** etc. will be strongly stressed but the second one will carry the normal weak stress.

1 She's buying bananas.
2 They're going to Rome.
3 He was eating fish and chips.
4 She's ordering chops.
5 They were living in England.
6 He's writing a novel.
7 They're drinking gin.
8 He's playing the trumpet.
9 She's dancing with Jack.
10 She's working for a stockbroker.
11 He was sitting beside Ann.
12 She's smoking a cigarette.
13 They're speaking Italian.
14 She's complaining about the food.
15 They were listening to the news.
16 They're coming back on Monday.
17 They're arriving at six.
18 She was picking apples.
19 He was looking for his sister.
20 She was lying on the floor.

48 Tenses: present simple and continuous, past continuous

☑ PEG 166, 173, 179

This is an exercise for three students. We shall call them **Jack**, **Tom** and **Mary**. **Jack** rings **Tom** at 5 a.m. and we hear the first part of this conversation. Later, say at 10 a.m., **Jack** mentions his call to **Mary**.

A: (*prompt only*) Polish my shoes.
JACK: Hello Tom! Are you in bed?
TOM: No. I'm polishing my shoes.
JACK: Do you always polish your shoes at 5 a.m.?

(*later*)
JACK: I rang Tom at 5 this morning.
MARY: Poor Tom. Was he in bed?
JACK: No. He was polishing his shoes.
MARY: What a funny time to polish shoes!

1 Tune the piano.
2 Cook breakfast.
3 Listen to the radio.
4 Take photographs.
5 Paint the ceiling.
6 Write poetry.
7 Practise the piano.
8 Do exercises.
9 Play cards.
10 Brush the dog.
11 Clean the windows.
12 Do my accounts. (*Use* **your** *in the answer.*)
13 Sew on my buttons. (*Use* **your** *in the answer.*)
14 Plan my next holiday. (*Use* **your** *in the answer.*)
15 Make jam.
16 Bake a cake.
17 Clean my room. (*Use* **your** *in the answer.*)
18 Peel potatoes.
19 Do a crossword puzzle. (*Use* **puzzles** *in the answer.*)
20 Repair my motorbike. (*Use* **your** *in the answer.*)

49 Tenses: negatives of the simple present, present continuous and simple past

☐   PEG 167, 173, 177

A: Do you finish at six?
B: *No, we don't finish till seven.*

A: Did she get home on Monday?
B: *No, she didn't get home till Tuesday.*

A: Are you starting in July?
B: *No we aren't starting till August.*

The time in the response should be an hour later or a day later or a week or a month later as appropriate.

1   Did you start at eight?
2   Did you arrive on the third?
3   Does the lesson begin at nine?
4   Do the shops shut at five?
5   Does he get up at seven?
6   Are you going on Wednesday?
7   Did he call you at six?
8   Is he leaving on Friday?
9   Did he pay you at the end of the first week?
10 Did he get there on the twenty-fourth?
11 Are they coming in July?
12 Do you expect to be ready by April?
13 Is the play being produced in May?
14 Does the post come at eight?
15 Are you starting your new job this week?
16 Are you seeing the solicitor on Thursday?
17 Did they report it on the first?
18 Was he arrested that day?
19 Did they operate on the fourth?
20 Are they releasing him today?

50 Tenses: present and past continuous with **always**

☑ PEG 167B, 180C

(a) A: Mike doesn't interrupt much, does he?
    B: *Oh yes, he does. He's always interrupting!* (stress on **always**)

    A: He doesn't change his job often, does he?
    B: *Oh yes, he does. He's always changing his job!* (stress on **always**)

(b) A: He didn't interrupt much, did he?
    B: *Oh yes, he did. He was always interrupting!* (stress on **always**)

    A: He didn't change his job often, did he?
    B: *Oh yes, he did. He was always changing his job!* (stress on **always**)

(a) *He doesn't . . . does he?*   (b) *He didn't . . . did he?*

1 smoke much
2 ask for help often
3 talk about her
4 argue much
5 often forget your telephone number (*Use* **my** *in the answer.*)
6 use the phone often
7 change his job often
8 have accidents often
9 get into trouble often
10 gossip much
11 boast often
12 break things often
13 look out of the window often
14 let you down often (*Use* **me** *in the answer.*)
15 grumble much
16 tell lies often
17 get into debt often
18 catch cold often
19 write to the newspapers
20 order you about much (*Use* **me** *in the answer.*)

51 Tenses: past continuous with **always** contrasted with simple past

☑ PEG 167B, 180C

A: He was always ringing!
B: *Nonsense! He only rang twice.*

A: He was always criticizing me!
B: *Nonsense! He only criticized you twice.*

He was always . . .

1 interrupting
2 complaining
3 interfering
4 changing his mind
5 losing his temper
6 getting drunk
7 breaking his promise
8 falling off (his horse)
9 waking me up
10 disappearing
11 going on strike
12 making a fuss
13 refusing (to help)
14 coming late (for work)
15 asking for a rise
16 shouting at me
17 leaving work early
18 taking her out
19 getting lost
20 oversleeping

52 Tenses: past simple and continuous

☑ PEG 177, 179

Prompt: Wash dishes.
A: What were you doing when you heard the crash?
B: *I was washing dishes.*
A: And what did you do when you heard it?
B: *I went on washing dishes.* (Or you could invent your own answer, provided you use the simple past tense.)

The prompts only are given as the questions are the same in each case.

1 listen to the radio
2 watch television
3 iron Tom's shirts
4 mend sheets
5 dye curtains
6 hang pictures
7 lay a carpet (*Use* the *in the second answer.*)
8 do exercises
9 write my diary
10 dust the sitting room
11 whitewash the passage
12 paint the bathroom door
13 tidy the bookshelves
14 arrange flowers
15 hang pictures
16 feed the goldfish
17 put things into the deep-freeze
18 take clothes out of the washing machine
19 make toast
20 stand on my head

53 Tenses: simple past pronunciation, **-ed** pronounced /ɪd/

☐

A: When did you report it?
B: *I reported it yesterday.*

When did . . .

1 he start?
2 she faint?
3 you expect him?
4 he invite her?
5 you remind them?
6 you wait for them?
7 she paint the door?
8 you want the information?
9 you need the advice?
10 you post the letters?
11 you dust the bedrooms?
12 you hand it in?
13 they appoint Peter?
14 they collect it?
15 you intend to start?
16 she accept the invitation?
17 she add these figures up?
18 they divide the takings?
19 he repeat his offer?
20 they decorate the Christmas tree?

54 Tenses: simple past pronunciation, **-ed** pronounced /t/

☐

A: Did you watch the match?
B: *Yes, of course I watched it.*

A: Did the lift stop?
B: *Yes, of course it stopped.*

1 Did you talk to them?
2 Did your scheme work?
3 Did they walk here?
4 Did he cook the steak?
5 Did she stuff the chicken?
6 Did the news astonish him?
7 Did he hope to see Ann?
8 Did they search the flat?
9 Did you dismiss him?
10 Did they kidnap the boy?
11 Did he cough?
12 Did you knock?
13 Did they tax his earnings?
14 Did he look for his passport?
15 Did she type the letters?
16 Did they discuss my suggestion?
17 Did the dogs bark?
18 Did you wrap it up?
19 Did they photograph the documents?
20 Did you laugh?

55 Tenses: simple past pronunciation, -ed pronounced /d/

☐

A: When did all this happen?
B: *It happened last week.*

A: When did he open your letters?
B: *He opened them last week.*

When did . . .

1 they move in?
2 the transmitter arrive?
3 they rewire the flat?
4 they install closed-circuit television?
5 the caretaker disappear?
6 they murder the other tenants?
7 they drug the landlord?
8 they dispose of the bodies?
9 they receive the stolen property?
10 they bury the gold bars?
11 they change the lock?
12 they oil the hinges?
13 they use the secret passage?
14 the leader threaten you?
15 the masked man follow you?
16 the neighbours complain?
17 you mention your suspicions?
18 you accuse them?
19 they destroy the evidence?
20 he erase the tapes?

56 Tenses: simple past pronunciation, mixed

☐

A: Did Ann complain?   A: Did Ann solve the problem?
B: *No. It was Tom who complained.*   B: *No. It was Tom who solved it.*

Did Ann . . .

1 apply for the job?
2 drop the eggs?
3 fix the tape recorder?
4 forward the letters?
5 organize the trip?
6 lock the safe?
7 wreck the car?
8 object?
9 accompany the students?
10 help Bill?
11 fetch the children?
12 suggest the party?
13 jump first?
14 land by parachute? (*Keep* **parachute.**)
15 ask you?
16 demand compensation? (*Keep* **compensation.**)
17 drug the coffee?
18 rescue you?
19 dictate these notes?
20 scream?

57 Tenses: simple past irregular verbs

☐ PEG chapter 39

A: You usually take two pieces of toast, don't you? (three)
B: *Yes, but today I took three.*

A: You usually buy your vegetables at your local greengrocer's, don't you? (the market)
B: *Yes, but today I bought them at the market.*

You usually . . . don't you?

1 get out at Leicester Square (Piccadilly)
2 drink water (wine)
3 meet Paul at his office (at his club)
4 feel well (awful)
5 read the Daily Telegraph (The Times)
6 send the documents by post (by hand)
7 tell Peter first (Janet)
8 go with Peter (with Paul)
9 come by bus (by taxi)
10 say too little (too much)
11 buy apples (pears)
12 stand at the side (at the back)
13 sit downstairs (upstairs)
14 leave at eight (at nine)
15 write three lines (three pages)
16 put the money in the safe (in the drawer)
17 ring her at seven (at six)
18 wake the children at eight (at seven)
19 spend a lot of money (hardly anything)
20 make a profit (a loss)

58 Tenses: simple past irregular verbs

☐ PEG chapter 39

A: Has he seen Ann?
B: *Yes, he saw her yesterday.*

A: Has he driven the car yet?
B: *Yes, he drove it yesterday.* (**yet** is omitted in the answer.)

1 Have you sold your car?
2 Have you spoken to Jack?
3 Have you lost your watch?
4 Have they heard the news?
5 Have they drunk the wine?
6 Have you rung Tom?
7 Has she seen the play?
8 Have you paid the bill?
9 Have you caught a fish yet? (*Use* **one** *in the answer.*)
10 Has she broken off the engagement? (*Note pronoun position: break* it *off.*)
11 Have you learnt your irregular verbs?
12 Has he torn his trousers?
13 Has he ever forgotten your birthday? (*No object is necessary. Omit* **ever**.)
14 Has she begun work yet? (*No object is necessary.*)
15 Have you found your keys?
16 Have you burnt the documents?
17 Has she swept the stairs?
18 Have you thrown the letter away? (*Note pronoun position: throw* it *away.*)
19 Have you given him the book? (*Note pronoun position: give* it *to* him.)
20 Have you ground the coffee?

59 Tenses: simple past interrogative

□ PEG 175, chapter 39

(i) A: I haven't seen Bill for ages.
    B: *When did you last see him?*

(ii) A: I haven't eaten an egg for ages.
     B: *When did you last eat one?*

I haven't . . . for ages.

1 drunk whisky
2 spoken German
3 read a book (*See* (*ii*) *above.*)
4 told a lie (*See* (*ii*) *above.*)
5 broken a glass (*See* (*ii*) *above.*)
6 written to Peter
7 had an accident (*See* (*ii*) *above.*)
8 made a mistake (*See* (*ii*) *above.*)
9 flown
10 driven a car (*See* (*ii*) *above.*)
11 ridden my motorbike
12 got lost
13 bought anything (*Use* **something**.)
14 cut my hair
15 kept him waiting (*Do not change* **waiting**.)
16 missed a class (*See* (*ii*) *above.*)
17 paid income tax
18 slept well
19 quarrelled with him
20 heard from her

60 Tenses: simple past, negative interrogative

☐ PEG 175, chapter 39

   A: I talked to Tom.
   B: *Didn't you talk to Jack too?*

1 I helped Bill.
2 I thanked George.
3 I paid Peter.
4 I congratulated Andrew.
5 I fined Paul.
6 I spoke to James.
7 I met Arthur.
8 I wrote to Bill.
9 I saw Ann.
10 I tipped Joan.
11 I photographed Oliver.
12 I sent a card to Hugh.
13 I got a ticket for Mary.
14 I kept a seat for Bob.
15 I asked George.
16 I invited Margaret.
17 I forgave Alec.
18 I offered a lift to Bill.
19 I stopped Peter.
20 I warned Hugh.

61 Tenses: **I thought you** + past tense

■

A: I go to work by bus. (tube)
B: *I thought you went to work by tube.*

1 I drink coffee. (tea)
2 He smokes cigars. (a pipe)
3 I leave home at 8.00. (9.00)
4 I start work at 9.00 (10.00)
5 I eat in the canteen. (in a restaurant)
6 I get up at 6.00. (7.00)
7 I make £40 a week. (£50)
8 He writes detective stories. (love stories)
9 The train leaves at 4.00. (4.30)
10 I spend £1 a week on fares. (£2)
11 I come from Scotland. (Wales)
12 I play tennis. (golf)
13 I collect coins. (stamps)
14 I agree with Peter. (Paul)
15 I always have lunch with Andrew. (George)
16 I paint in water-colours. (oils)
17 I need a hammer. (chisel)
18 He prefers Ann. (Mary)
19 I cook it in butter. (oil)
20 He sells tape recorders. (radios)

62 Tenses: **I thought you** + past tense

◪

(a) A: I live in Kensington.
   B: *I thought you lived in Pimlico.*

Keep the nouns unchanged.

1 I work in Mayfair.
2 I shop in Kensington.
3 I live in Finchley.
4 I go to classes in Soho.
5 I leave my car in Victoria.
6 Peter and I meet in Hyde Park.
7 I send his mail to Westminster.
8 I get out at Brixton.
9 I catch my train at Earl's Court.
10 I buy my shoes in Knightsbridge.
11 I play tennis in Dulwich.
12 I prefer Vauxhall.
13 I want a garage in Barnet.
14 I spend my weekends in Whitechapel.
15 He refuses to live in Lambeth.

(b) A: I teach English.
   B: *Oh, I thought you taught French.*

1 I speak English in class.
2 I correct his English.
3 I sing in English.
4 I write the minutes of the meeting in English.
5 I complain in English.
6 I argue in English.
7 I test their English.
8 I shout at him in English.
9 I translate the letters into English.
10 I give the instructions in English.
11 I explain in English.
12 I swear in English.
13 I think in English.
14 I count in English.
15 We discuss it in English.

63 Tenses: **I didn't know** + past tense

■

A: These are my skis.
B: *I didn't know you skied.*

A: George keeps his chess set
here. (play)
B: *I didn't know he played chess.*

1 These are my knitting needles.
2 These are Ann's skates.
3 Here are Tom's boxing gloves.
4 This is Mary's fishing rod.
5 This is Bill's fencing mask.
6 These are Ann's paintbrushes.
7 Here are George's water-skis.
8 This is Paul's diving equipment.
9 These are my sailing clothes.
10 These are Mary's gardening gloves.
11 Here are Tom's football boots. (play)
12 George keeps his cigars in that drawer. (smoke)
13 Those crash-helmets over there belong to the boys. (ride motorbikes)
14 Here's my stamp album. (collect)
15 These are photos of me flying helicopters.
16 I'm looking for my contact lenses. (wear)
17 All this mountain-climbing equipment belongs to Hugo. (climb)
18 Here are some photos of me making speeches at Hyde Park Corner.
19 Here are some photos of me leading demonstrations.
20 I keep my fortune-telling equipment in that cupboard. (tell fortunes)

64 Tenses: present perfect

☑ PEG 183

A: I suppose you met Tom some time ago.
B: *No, I've only just met him.*

I suppose . . . some time ago.

1 you heard this (*Use* it *for* this.)
2 he arrived
3 she left
4 they got engaged
5 she arranged this (*Use* it.)
6 she accepted your suggestion
7 they bought the house
8 he told her
9 the course began
10 the shop opened
11 he suggested this (*Use* it.)
12 you and Tom enrolled
13 he passed his test
14 you signed the lease
15 they cancelled their booking
16 he resigned
17 they emigrated
18 they arrested him
19 he answered
20 you booked the seats

65 Tenses: present perfect

☑ PEG 192

A: I've been picking pears.
B: *How* many *have you picked?*

A: He's been making a lot of money.
B: *How* much *has he made?*

Note that if the things that are being talked about are countable, you should use *many*. If they are uncountable, you should use *much*.

1 I've been planting apple trees.
2 I've been making cakes.
3 He's been cleaning shoes.
4 He's been writing letters.
5 We've been mending sheets.
6 I've been washing blankets.
7 I've been applying for jobs.
8 I've been taking photographs.
9 I've been saving money.
10 Tom has been putting on weight.
11 Ann's been losing weight.
12 Peter's been answering advertisements.
13 Mary's been sending out invitations.
14 I've been cutting sandwiches.
15 George has been painting pictures.
16 Tom has been looking at houses.
17 I've been addressing envelopes.
18 I've been ironing shirts.
19 I've been grinding coffee.
20 I've been peeling onions.

66 Tenses: present perfect

☑ PEG 185

A: When did you last write to Peter?
B: *Oh, I haven't written to him for ages.*

A: When did you last ride a camel?
B: *Oh, I haven't ridden one for ages.*

(When the object has the form: **a/an** + a noun, use **one** in the answer.)

When did . . .

1 you last see Tom?
2 you last make a bad mistake?
3 you and Bill last eat out?
4 he last do a good day's work?
5 you last sleep well?
6 she last read a book?
7 he last take part in a competition?
8 you last hear from them?
9 you last fly a plane?
10 you last speak to Bill?
11 he last teach?
12 he last pay you?
13 he last write to you?
14 you last go to the theatre?
15 you last catch a fish?
16 he last shave?
17 he last have a job?
18 you last sell a picture?
19 you and Peter last discuss this matter?
20 you last win a race?

67 Tenses: present perfect continuous

■ PEG 191

A: I live here.
B: *How long have you been living here?*

A: I'm looking for a job.
B: *How long have you been looking for a job?*

Keep the nouns unchanged.

1 I work here.
2 I'm learning Greek.
3 I'm waiting for Peter.
4 I sleep badly.
5 I'm economizing.
6 He drives a bus.
7 I check their accounts.
8 I pay his school fees.
9 He cooks.
10 She does two jobs.
11 I feel depressed.
12 He's blackmailing me.
13 He sends anonymous letters.
14 I collect fossils.
15 He receives stolen goods.
16 They meet secretly.
17 I'm losing weight.
18 I help Peter with his homework.
19 I live in a condemned house.
20 They are squatting in an empty block.

68 Tenses: past perfect

☑ PEG 194B, 195

A: Were you in time to stop Tom telling Ann?
B: *No, when I arrived he'd just told her.*

Were you in time to stop Tom . . .

1 posting the letter?
2 resigning?
3 accepting the conditions?
4 ringing Ann?
5 signing the contract?
6 confessing?
7 admitting his guilt?
8 refusing the job?
9 leaving?
10 taking the pills?
11 buying the shares?
12 selling his car?
13 cancelling the booking?
14 telling his boss?
15 showing the letter to the police?
16 proposing to Mary?
17 starting?
18 cutting the tree down?
19 burning the documents?
20 shooting his wife?

69 Tenses: past perfect continuous

◪ PEG 197

A: When you met him had he just started following her?
B: *No, he'd been following her for some time.*

Keep the nouns unchanged.

When you met him had he just started . . .

1 receiving stolen goods?
2 selling information?
3 stealing the petty cash?
4 photographing the secret documents?
5 forging his employer's signature?
6 cooking the books?
7 avoiding income tax?
8 drinking?
9 taking drugs?
10 following you about?
11 watching the house?
12 opening her mail?
13 recording your conversations? (*Use* **my** *in the answer.*)
14 threatening his tenants?
15 gambling?
16 losing money?
17 telling lies?
18 betting heavily?
19 cheating his customers?
20 going downhill?

70 Future forms: present continuous

☑ PEG 202, 308

(a)
A: Have you decided when to go?
B: *Yes, we're going on Tuesday.*

A: Have you decided when to meet Tom?
B: *Yes, we're meeting him on Tuesday*

(b)
A: What did he say about going?
B: *He said they were going on Tuesday.*

A: What did he say about Tom?
B: *He said they were meeting him on Tuesday.*

The two groups of exercises could be worked through separately, or they could be combined with students working in pairs. e.g.
A: Have you decided when to go?
FIRST STUDENT: *Yes, we're going on Tuesday.*
A: What did he say about going?
SECOND STUDENT: *He said they were going on Tuesday.*

(a) *Have you decided when to . . .*

1 leave?
2 start?
3 set off?
4 move out?
5 come back?
6 return?
7 demonstrate?
8 march?
9 take the test?
10 announce your engagement?
11 interview the candidates?
12 test the new model?
13 open the new branch?
14 launch the ship?
15 meet Peter?
16 inspect the premises?
17 invite your parents?
18 see the bank manager?
19 hire the car?
20 make your speech?

(b) *What did he say about . . .*

1 leaving?
2 starting?
3 setting off?
4 moving out?
5 coming back?
6 returning?
7 demonstrating?
8 marching?
9 the test?
10 their engagement?
11 the candidates?
12 the new model?
13 the new branch?
14 the ship?
15 Peter?
16 the premises?
17 his parents?
18 the bank manager?
19 the car?
20 his speech?

71

71 Future forms: **will** contrasted with present continuous

■ PEG 201, 202

The students of a college are planning a party. The organizer asks for volunteers to do the various jobs in connection with this.
(a) A: The hall must be cleaned.
   B: *I'll clean the hall.* (Keep the nouns unchanged.)

Later, someone asks what arrangements have been made:
(b) A: What about the hall? (Peter)
   B: *Peter is cleaning it.*
   (Replace noun objects by pronouns. Be careful with numbers 2, 3, 18 and 19 as here the combinations require a change of word order, e.g. *Bring back* the glasses but: *Bring them back.*)

(a)	(b) *What about . . .*
1 The Principal must be told.	1 the Principal? (Tom)
2 Invitations must be sent out.	2 the invitations? (Ann)
3 Notices must be put up.	3 the notices? (Jack)
4 The floor must be swept.	4 the floor? (Mary)
5 The windows must be cleaned.	5 the windows? (Alec)
6 The tables must be laid.	6 the tables? (Bill)
7 Glasses must be hired.	7 the glasses? (Joan)
8 Sandwiches must be cut.	8 the sandwiches? (Alice)
9 The wine must be ordered.	9 the wine? (Peter)
10 The bottles must be opened.	10 the bottles? (Bill)
11 The coffee must be made.	11 the coffee? (Hilda)
12 Milk and sugar must be brought.	12 the milk and sugar? (Vera)
13 A disc jockey must be hired.	13 the disc jockey? (Andrew)
14 The guests' coats must be looked after.	14 the guests' coats? (Hugh)
15 The parking must be supervised.	15 the parking? (George)
16 Records must be borrowed.	16 the records? (Jill)
17 Accounts must be kept.	17 the accounts? (Michael)
18 The empties must be taken back.	18 the empties? (Rupert)
19 The dirty dishes must be washed up.	19 the dirty dishes? (Brian)
20 The caretaker must be tipped.	20 the caretaker? (John)

72 Future forms: **will** used at moment of decision

☑ PEG 201

Evening conversation:

(a) A: You washed the car, didn't you?
   B: *I'm afraid I forgot! But I'll wash it tomorrow.*

(b) Later that evening someone else asks:
   A: She washed the car, didn't she?
   B: *No, she forgot. But she said she'd wash it tomorrow.*

(a) *You . . . , didn't you?*

1 told Peter
2 rang Ann
3 asked Jack
4 reminded Bill
5 paid Alexander
6 thanked Mary
7 helped the twins
8 booked the seats
9 got the licence
10 answered the letter
11 swept the stairs
12 apologized to Peter
13 invited the Smiths
14 burnt the rubbish
15 wound the clock
16 took the books back
17 bought the tickets
18 made the list
19 checked the brakes
20 insured the car

(b) *She . . . , didn't she?*

1 told Peter
2 rang Ann
   etc., exactly as in (a).

Note that:
She said she'd wash it tomorrow
could be replaced by
She's washing it tomorrow
(= this has been decided or
arranged) or
*She is going to wash it
tomorrow*
(= this is her intention).

73 Future forms: **going to**

■ PEG 204

A: Have you changed your mind about selling your house?
B: *No, I'm going to sell it.*

Have you changed your mind about . . .

1 applying for the job?
2 telling the police?
3 complaining about the delay?
4 reporting Smith?
5 buying a car? (*Use* **one.**)
6 hiring a television set? (*Use* **one.**)
7 recording the conversation?
8 paying the fine?
9 raising his salary?
10 employing her?
11 warning them?
12 writing to Brian?
13 repairing the car?
14 inviting the Smiths?
15 sending Tom?
16 selling your yacht?
17 accepting his offer?
18 having the party at home?
19 building a garage? (*Use* **one.**)
20 letting the top flat?

74 Future forms: **going to** negative

☑ PEG 204

Sunday evening conversation between husband and wife:
WIFE: You brought me tea in bed yesterday. (Keep **tea** and **bed**.)
HUSBAND: *Yes, but I'm not going to bring you tea in bed tomorrow.*

WIFE: You cooked the breakfast yesterday.
HUSBAND: *Yes, but I'm not going to cook it tomorrow.*

Use pronoun objects unless otherwise instructed.

You . . . yesterday.

1 got up first
2 ground the coffee
3 made the toast
4 washed up
5 left the car at home
6 let me drive
7 rang me from the office (*Omit* **from the office.**)
8 came straight home after work (*Omit* **after work.**)
9 brought me flowers (*Keep* **flowers.**)
10 did the shopping for me
11 bathed the baby
12 played with the children
13 repaired Ann's bicycle
14 blew up Tom's football (*Watch the word order.*)
15 read to the children
16 mowed the grass
17 watered the roses
18 helped me wash up
19 invited my mother round for a drink (*Omit* **for a drink.**)
20 babysat while I went out with my mother (*Omit* **while . . . mother.**)

75 Future forms: future tense

☑ PEG 209

A: Is Tom bringing his dogs?
B: *He hasn't said anything, but I suppose he'll bring them.*

1 Are they inviting Ann?
2 Is Peter paying for the dinner?
3 Is Hugh applying for the job?
4 Is Arthur having the operation?
5 Are the Smiths selling their car?
6 Are the Joneses letting their top flat?
7 Is Peter resigning?
8 Is the company taking on more staff? (*Leave* **more staff** *unchanged.*)
9 Is Ann flying?
10 Are your students re-enrolling?
11 Is your brother going abroad?
12 Is Peter entering for the exam?
13 Are your sisters speaking (at next week's debate?) (*Omit the words in brackets.*)
14 Is Paul playing (in the tournament next month)? (*Omit the words in brackets.*)
15 Are your parents staying (abroad) for some time? (*Omit the words in brackets.*)
16 Is Hugo coming back (to England)? (*Omit the words in brackets.*)
17 Is Vera going on with her course?
18 Are they getting married soon?
19 Is Tom taking his wife with him?
20 Are they celebrating their silver wedding?

This exercise could also be done with: **I expect he'll/I hope he'll/he'll probably/perhaps he'll.**

76 Future forms: future continuous

■ PEG 211

A: Paul's on holiday; he's having a marvellous time.
B: *This time next week I'll be having a marvellous time too.* (stress on I'll)

I shall is the technically correct form here, but **I will/I'll** is more often heard.

Keep the nouns unchanged.

Paul's on holiday; he's . . .

1 sunbathing.
2 having breakfast in bed.
3 drinking fresh grapejuice.
4 winning money at the casino.
5 surf-riding.
6 skin-diving.
7 tunny-fishing.
8 taking photos under water.
9 relaxing in a deck chair.
10 swinging in a hammock.
11 water ski-ing.
12 meeting all sorts of exciting people.
13 eating exotic dishes.
14 going for moonlight bathes.
15 bargaining for souvenirs.
16 riding across the desert.
17 camping under the palm trees.
18 sleeping under the stars.
19 buying presents for everybody.
20 wishing he hadn't to come home. (*stress on the second* 'I')

77

77 Future forms: future continuous interrogative

☑ PEG 211

A: I usually see Ann on Mondays.
B: *Will you be seeing her next Monday?* (stress on **next**)

I usually . . .

1 let my house in August.
2 lunch with Bill on Monday.
3 leave early on Friday.
4 go camping in summer.
5 have a drink with Jack on Tuesday. (*Keep* **drink.**)
6 give Mary a lift home on Wednesday. (*Keep* **a lift home.**)
7 play golf on Sunday.
8 ring Sam on Saturday.
9 take Ann out on Monday.
10 sail on Saturday.
11 watch television on Sunday evening. (*Keep* **television.**)
12 take the dogs for a walk at the weekend.
13 listen to the radio on Sunday morning.
14 write to my father on Thursday.
15 type the reports on Friday.
16 do my accounts on Saturday.
17 change my library book on Thursday.
18 meet Arthur on Tuesday.
19 dine out on Friday.
20 visit my mother-in-law on Wednesday.

78 Future forms: future continuous negative

■ PEG 211

A: Ann usually arranges the flowers.
B: *She won't be arranging the flowers tomorrow; she's just been given the day off.*

Keep the nouns unchanged.

Ann usually . . .

1 opens the mail.
2 dusts the boss's desk.
3 answers the phone.
4 does the translating.
5 deals with dissatisfied customers.
6 receives new clients.
7 takes shorthand notes.
8 writes the minutes.
9 types the reports.
10 files the copies.
11 makes the tea.
12 brings the tea round.
13 addresses the letters.
14 arranges the boss's interviews.
15 checks the petty cash.
16 programmes the computer.
17 pays the staff.
18 works out the tax.
19 operates the photocopier.
20 turns out the lights.

79 Future forms: **will** + continuous infinitive

■ PEG 213

Ann's day:

6.30 –	7.00	gets dressed	4.00 –	4.30	gives children their tea
7.00 –	7.30	dresses the baby			
7.30 –	8.00	cooks breakfast	4.30 –	5.30	helps the children with their homewoɪ
8.00 –	8.30	has breakfast			
8.30 –	9.00	takes the children to school	5.30 –	6.00	picks up her husbaɪ at the station
9.00 – 11.00		does housework	6.00 –	6.30	reads to the childre
11.00 – 11.30		reads paper	6.30 –	7.00	puts the baby to be
11.30 – 12.30		shops	7.00 –	7.30	cooks supper
12.30 –	1.00	cooks lunch	7.30 –	8.30	has supper
1.00 –	2.00	has lunch	8.30 –	9.00	washes up after supper
2.00 –	2.30	writes letters			
2.30 –	3.30	takes the dogs for a walk	9.00 – 11.00		talks/reads/watcheɪ TV etc.
3.30 –	4.00	collects the children from school	11.00 – 11.30		goes to bed

(a)

A: It's 6.45. I wonder what Ann's doing now.

B: *Oh, she'll be getting dressed.*

(**will** here is used for assumption.)

It's . . . I wonder what Ann's doing now.

1	7.15	11	3.00
2	7.45	12	3.45
3	8.15	13	4.15
4	8.45	14	4.45
5	10.00	15	5.45
6	11.15	16	6.15
7	12.00	17	6.45
8	12.45	18	7.15
9	1.30	19	8.00
10	2.15	20	8.45

(b)

A: Shall I ring Ann at 6.45 tomorrow?

B: *No, don't ring then. She'll be getting dressed.*

(**will** here is used for the future.)

Shall I ring Ann at . . . tomorrow?

1	7.15	11	5.45
2	7.45	12	6.45
3	8.15	13	7.15
4	8.45	14	7.45
5	12.00	15	11.15
6	12.45		
7	1.30		
8	3.00		
9	3.45		
10	4.15		

80 Future forms: **will** + perfect infinitive

■ PEG 160B

This is also based on the programme given with the previous exercise.

A: It's 7.45. Will Ann still be dressing the baby?
B: *No, she'll have dressed him by now.* (**will** here is used for assumption.)

It's . . . Will Ann still be . . . ?

1 8.15 . . . cooking breakfast
2 8.45 . . . having breakfast
3 9.15 . . . taking the children to school (*Omit* **to school.**)
4 11.45 . . . doing the housework
5 2.45 . . . writing her letters
6 3.45 . . . walking the dogs
7 4.15 . . . collecting the children from school (*Omit* **from school.**)
8 4.45 . . . giving the children their tea (*Watch the word order.*)
9 5.45 . . . helping the children with their homework
10 6.15 . . . picking up her husband (*Watch the word order.*)
11 6.45 . . . reading to the children
12 7.15 . . . putting the baby to bed
13 8.15 . . . cooking supper
14 9.15 . . . washing up
15 11.45 . . . going to bed

81 Future forms: future perfect

■ PEG 216

A: It'll take you ages to paint all these chairs, won't it?
B: *No, I'll have painted them all by the end of the week.*

Note 1   By using this tense the speaker implies that he will not have to make a special effort to be finished by the end of the week. If he works at his normal rate he will be finished.

I will paint them all by the end of the week would also be possible, but would indicate that the speaker intended or promised to do this. It might imply that he would make a special effort to be ready in time.

Note 2   *I shall have painted* is the technically correct form, but *I will/ I'll have painted* is more often heard.

It'll take you ages to . . . , won't it?

1 paint all the doors
2 change all the fuses
3 rewire all the flats
4 lay all the new carpets
5 wash all the curtains
6 hang all these pictures
7 repaper the top rooms
8 clear all the blocked drains
9 varnish all the woodwork
10 weed the flower beds
11 mow all the grass
12 patch all these pillow cases
13 iron all these sheets
14 plant all these bulbs
15 sow all these seeds
16 replace all these tiles
17 scrub all these stairs
18 polish all this silver
19 pick all these apples
20 bottle all this wine

82 Future forms: future perfect continuous

■ PEG 216

A: Have you just started chicken farming?
B: *Oh no. By the end of the month I'll have been chicken farming for five*
   years. (*I shall* is the technically correct form here, but *I will/I'll* is
   more often heard.)

Have you just started . . .

1 collecting stamps?
2 bird-watching?
3 keeping hens?
4 painting?
5 playing the violin?
6 sailing?
7 complaining?
8 looking for gold?
9 going to meetings?
10 writing to the papers?
11 growing roses?
12 selling peaches?
13 translating documents?
14 telling fortunes?
15 flying jets?
16 reading The Times?
17 making jam?
18 going to work by boat?
19 working for Bill?
20 riding a motorbike?

83 Conditional sentences type 1 and time clauses

☑ PEG 221, 342

A: You'll tell Tom, won't you?
(a) B: *Well, if I see him I'll tell him.*
A: What did you say?
(b) B: *I said if I saw him I'd tell him.*

Alternatively time clauses can be used:
A: You'll tell Tom, won't you?
(c) B: *Yes, I'll tell him as soon as he comes in.*
A: What did you say?
(d) B: *I said I'd tell him as soon as he came in.*

Note When there is a double object e.g. *You'll give* Peter *the* message, *won't you?*, use **to** and change the object order: *Well, if I see him I'll give* it *to* him.

You'll . . . won't you?

1 ask Peter
2 thank John
3 pay Ann
4 remind Mary
5 warn the children
6 tell them
7 apologize to George
8 kiss him
9 congratulate them
10 invite her
11 discuss it with George
12 explain the situation to Mary
13 show Peter the photographs (*See note above.*)
14 give Ann the money (*See note.*)
15 recommend it to Alec
16 suggest it to Peter
17 offer Bill the money (*See note.*)
18 point it out to Bob
19 speak to Mary
20 hand Hugo this letter (*See note.*)

84 Conditional sentences: type 1

☑ PEG 221

A: Perhaps he'll refuse.
B: *Well, if he refuses please let me know.*

Keep noun objects unchanged.

Perhaps he'll . . .

1 complain.
2 ask for more money.
3 go on strike.
4 object.
5 make a fuss.
6 threaten me.
7 demand an explanation.
8 try to bribe me.
9 accuse me.
10 blame me.
11 refuse to co-operate.
12 want proof.
13 report me to the police.
14 take my passport away.
15 make conditions.
16 argue.
17 insist on a written agreement.
18 hi-jack my plane.
19 kidnap me.
20 shoot at me.

85 Conditional sentences: type 1

☑ PEG 221, 226

A: Ann thinks Paul will probably start tomorrow.
B: *But unless he starts today he'll be too late.*

Ann thinks Paul will probably . . . tomorrow.

1 come
2 begin
3 decide
4 sign
5 apply
6 leave
7 send it
8 post it
9 tell us
10 set out
11 book the seats
12 pay
13 claim it
14 report it
15 arrive
16 enrol
17 go
18 accept
19 fly
20 arrange it

86 Conditional sentences: type 2

☑ PEG 222

A: I suppose I'll have to ask someone else to put me up.
B: *I'm afraid so. I'd put you up if I could but I can't.*

I suppose I'll have to ask someone else to . . .

1 meet me.
2 see me off.
3 help me.
4 wait for me.
5 keep me a place. (*Leave* **place** *unchanged.*)
6 show me the way. (*Leave* **way** *unchanged.*)
7 fix it for me.
8 translate it.
9 give me a lift. (*Leave* **lift** *unchanged.*)
10 carry it for me.
11 find me a job. (*Leave* **job** *unchanged.*)
12 go with me.
13 babysit.
14 take over.
15 do it.
16 arrange it for me.
17 drive me.
18 explain it to me.
19 show me how to do it.
20 advise me.

87 Conditional sentences: type 2

☑ PEG 222

A: He lives near his work so he's always in time.
B: *If* I *lived near my work* I'd *always be in time too.* (Stress the subjects.) [**should** is also possible]

A: His case is light so he carries it himself.
B: *If* my *case were light* I'd *carry it myself too.* (Stress **my** and 'I'.)

A: Tom and his wife have a colour television so they stay at home in the evenings.
B: *If we had a colour television we'd stay at home in the evenings too.*

1 She is nice and slim, so she looks marvellous in tight jeans.
2 He has plenty of money, so he spends the winters abroad.
3 He works overtime, so he earns a lot of money.
4 His garden gets a lot of sun, so he can grow peaches.
5 He can ski, so he goes skiing at Christmas.
6 They use electric typewriters, so they finish early.
7 She knows a film director, so she gets good parts.
8 She gets two hours for lunch, so she goes to lunch-time concerts.
9 Both Jack and his wife work, so they can afford expensive holidays. (**if we . . .**)
10 He reads the newspapers carefully and always knows what's happening.
11 He runs round the park every morning, so he keeps very fit.
12 He travels first class, so he enjoys travelling.
13 Mrs Jones employs an au pair girl, so she can spend all day reading novels.
14 His alarm clock rings very loudly, so he always wakes up in time.
15 Her husband leaves the car at home, so she goes shopping in it.
16 They do their own decorating, so they save a lot of money. (**if we . . .**)
17 He belongs to a club, so he meets a lot of people.
18 He meets a lot of people, so he makes a lot of friends.
19 She has everything she wants, so she is perfectly happy.
20 He understands electricity so he does his own repairs.

88 Conditional sentences: type 2 using the continuous infinitive

■ PEG 222C

A: Tom's on holiday now; I expect he's sitting on the beach.
B: *If I were on holiday I'd be sitting on the beach too.* (stress on both 'I's)

(Technically **should** is the correct form here, but **would** ('d) is more often heard.)

Tom's on holiday now; I expect he's . . .

1 pony-trekking.
2 sailing.
3 gardening.
4 lying in a hammock.
5 fishing.
6 camping.
7 sight-seeing.
8 playing tennis.
9 swimming.
10 sitting on the beach.
11 sitting in a deckchair.
12 mowing the lawn.
13 skin-diving.
14 painting pictures.
15 watching a football match.
16 touring Italy.
17 buying antiques.
18 taking photographs.
19 sun-bathing.
20 driving along a motorway.

89 Conditional sentences: type 3

■ PEG 223

A: Why didn't you pay Tom?
B: *You didn't tell me to. If you'd told me to, I'd have paid him of course.*

Why didn't you . . .

1 wait for Henry?
2 meet John?
3 thank James?
4 warn Mary?
5 remind the children?
6 invite Mr and Mrs Jones?
7 ring Margaret?
8 send the parcel?
9 phone the doctor?
10 write to George?
11 report it?
12 ask Billy?
13 propose Peter?
14 sack Tom?
15 look for Philip?
16 follow the man?
17 search the house?
18 vote for Donald?
19 stop the car?
20 oppose the new policy?

90 Conditional sentences: type 3

■ PEG 223

(i) A: He didn't ask me to go.
    B: *Would you have gone if he had asked you?* (slight stress on **had**)

(ii) A: He didn't ask me to open the letters.
    B: *Would you have opened them if he had asked you?*

(iii) A: He didn't ask me to send him the papers.
    B: *Would you have sent them to him if he had asked you?* (Note word order.)

He didn't ask me to . . .

1 wait for him.
2 help him.
3 see him off.
4 show him my notes. (*See (iii) above.*)
5 lend it to him.
6 paint his portrait.
7 open the safe.
8 photograph the documents.
9 iron his shirts.
10 write to him.
11 explain.
12 pay.
13 move the car.
14 do it again.
15 type the report.
16 give him the key. (*See (iii) above.*)
17 change my plans.
18 keep it a secret.
19 marry him.
20 contribute.

91 Conditional sentences: type 3

■ PEG 223

(a) A: I didn't feel well; that's why I didn't go with him.
    B: *So if you'd felt well you'd have gone with him, would you?*

1 I hadn't the paper qualifications so I didn't get the post.
2 I didn't do the last question so I didn't pass.
3 I didn't know his number so I didn't ring him.
4 I didn't take his threats seriously so I didn't tell the police.
5 He didn't finish the job so I didn't pay him.
6 I didn't realize he was ill so I didn't give him the day off.
7 My gun wasn't loaded so I didn't fire.
8 My wife didn't encourage me, that's why I didn't get to the top.
9 They didn't give me a work permit so I didn't stay here.
10 I didn't hear him knocking so I didn't open the door.

(b) A: He didn't tell me the lions were loose, so I left the car.
    B: *So if he had told you the lions were loose you wouldn't have left the car, eh?*

1 I didn't know I was overdrawn so I gave them a cheque.
2 I wasn't given correct information so I arrived at a false conclusion.
3 They didn't shut the loading door properly; that's why the plane crashed.
4 He didn't love her; that's why he deceived her.
5 I didn't know the whole story so I blamed Tom.
6 They hadn't enough lifeboats; that's why there was such loss of life.
7 He couldn't swim; that's why he was drowned.
8 He didn't tie up the boat so it drifted away.
9 I didn't realize the lion was dangerous so I opened the cage.
10 I didn't expect him to ring back at once so I went out.

92 I wish + past tense/If only + past tense

☑ PEG 228, 300

(a) A: Can you type?
   B: *No I can't. I wish I could.* (Or: *If only I could!*)

The **if only** form is much more dramatic and less generally useful than the **I wish** form.

1 Is she flying?
2 Can you drive a car?
3 Do you know where we are?
4 Have you got a map?
5 Are your children with you?
6 Does he come straight home after work?
7 Are your students interested in languages?
8 Is it your weekend off?
9 Can you understand this notice?
10 Have you done your packing?

(b) A: Do they eat sweets between meals?
   B: *Yes, they do. I wish they didn't.* (Or: *If only they didn't.*)

   A: Need/Must you go?
   B: *Yes, I must. I wish I didn't have to.*

Use **didn't have to** to express negative obligation.

1 Are your friends leaving tomorrow?
2 Does he smoke in bed?
3 Must you start tomorrow?
4 Are they selling their house?
5 Do they want to emigrate?
6 Have you signed the contract?
7 Is he going out tonight?
8 Need you appear in court?
9 Have you posted the letter?
10 Must you do military service?

93 I wish + past tense/If only + past tense

■ PEG 228, 300

A: I'm going by air.
B: *I wish I was going by air.* (stress on the second 'I')

A: I've passed my test.
B: *I wish I'd passed my test.* (stress on the second 'I' and on **my**)

or
If only I was going by air!
If only I had passed my test!
(This form is much more dramatic and less generally useful than the I wish form.)

Keep nouns unchanged.

1 I have a flat here.
2 I know five languages.
3 I live near my work.
4 I can park outside my office.
5 My case is quite light.
6 I'm getting thinner.
7 I have six weeks' holiday a year.
8 My son writes every week.
9 My boss hands out free theatre tickets.
10 I've worked hard all the year.
11 I get the weekends off.
12 I have plenty of time for reading.
13 My neighbours are very quiet.
14 I get a bonus at Christmas.
15 I find it easy to concentrate.
16 I understand it.
17 I can take a day off any time.
18 I've saved £100.
19 My house looks out on a park.
20 My parents give me an allowance.

94 I wish + past perfect and If only + past perfect

☑ PEG 228, 300

(a) A: I asked Bill.
    B: *I wish you'd asked Tom too.* (**had** is normally contracted here.)
    or: *If only you'd asked Tom too!*

1 I paid Jack.
2 I invited Paul.
3 I scolded Peter.
4 I stoppped Mary.
5 I rang Ann.
6 I wrote to Alec.
7 I voted for Bill.
8 I suggested Arthur.
9 I spoke to John.
10 I warned Philip.

(b) A: I only left an umbrella.
    B: *I wish you hadn't left anything.* (slight stress on **anything**)
    or: *If only you hadn't left anything!* (slight stress on **anything**)
    A: I only paid the guide.
    B: *I wish you hadn't paid anyone.* (slight stress on **anyone**)
    or: *If only you hadn't paid anyone!* (slight stress on **anyone**)

I only . . .

1 said a few words.
2 ate a few nuts.
3 drank half a glass of wine.
4 tipped the porter.
5 gave 10p.
6 signed the bill.
7 photographed the entrance.
8 admitted one thing.
9 took an apple.
10 told Andrew.

95 Requests

☐ PEG 284

    A: Ask me to shut the door.
(a) B: *Would you shut the door, please?*
(b) B: *Could you shut the door, please?*

Ask me to . . .

1 tell Jack.
2 ask Mary.
3 ring Ann.
4 turn off the light.
5 lock the door.
6 come in quietly.
7 write at once.
8 thank him.
9 forward your letters.
10 go myself.
11 mend the fuse.
12 cancel the papers.
13 pay the milkman.
14 let me know about this.
15 give him his lunch.
16 feed the goldfish.
17 water the roses.
18 answer the letter.
19 cook the lunch.
20 send him a cheque.

96 Requests

☐ PEG 284

    A: Ask me to join the queue.

(a) B: *If you'd join the queue.*
    (This is a fairly casual form of request only used when the request is very reasonable and there is no chance of objection.)

(b) B: *Would you like to join the queue?*
    (**would you** and **could you** would be equally possible here, but for convenience we will restrict the exercises to **if you'd** and **would you like to**)

Ask me to . . .

1 open my case.
2 sign here.
3 give you some proof of my identity.
4 put my name and address on the back of the cheque.
5 show you my passport.
6 wait in the waiting room.
7 ring this number.
8 write to this address.
9 leave my name and telephone number.
10 take off my coat.
11 open my book at page 60.
12 go up to the next floor.
13 come this way.
14 fill up this form.
15 follow you.
16 pay the cashier.
17 accompany you to the manager's office.
18 tell you exactly what happened.
19 have a look at these brochures.
20 think it over.

97 Requests: **Would you mind** + gerund

☑ PEG 263, 284D, K

    A: Have the windows been cleaned?
(a) B: *No. Would you mind cleaning them?*
(b) B: *No. I wonder if you'd mind cleaning them.*

Have/has the . . .

1 beds been made?
2 table been laid?
3 stairs been swept?
4 coffee been ground?
5 onions been cut up?
6 washing-up been done?
7 gas bill been paid?
8 steps been scrubbed?
9 furniture been polished?
10 dining room been dusted?
11 shopping been done?
12 sheets been ironed?
13 tea been made?
14 laundry been collected?
15 clock been wound?
16 cheese been grated?
17 letters been posted.
18 sandwiches been cut?
19 potatoes been peeled?
20 chips been fried?

98 Requests: **Would you mind if . . .** and **Would it be all right if . . .**

☑ PEG 263

A: I'd like you to go today.
(a) B: *Would you mind if I went tomorrow instead?*
(*Would you mind if I go* is also possible, but the past tense is better after **would**. *Do you mind if I go* is also possible, but more casual. **would you mind** is more polite.)
(b) B: *Would it be all right if I went tomorrow instead?*

I'd like you to . . . today.

1 leave
2 ring the Smiths
3 tell Jack
4 pay the bill
5 write to Mary
6 send the cheque
7 buy the tickets
8 begin
9 report it
10 mend it
11 make the cake
12 change the wheel
13 check the brakes
14 renew your licence
15 do your packing
16 book the seats
17 decide
18 move out
19 make the inventory
20 settle the account

99 Expressions of preference: would rather/would prefer to

☑ PEG 297

    A: Would you like to go with Peter or with Paul?
(a) B: *I'd rather go with Paul.*
(b) B: *I'd prefer to go with Paul.*

    A: Would you like to fry it or grill it?
(a) B: *I'd rather grill it.*
(b) B: *I'd prefer to grill it.*

Would you like to . . .

1 have supper at home or go out to supper?
2 join a nine o'clock class or an eleven o'clock class?
3 drive or fly?
4 pay cash or by cheque?
5 marry a poor man or a rich man?
6 stay at home after marriage or go out to work?
7 write to him or ring him?
8 eat it raw or cook it?
9 watch cricket or tennis?
10 see a film or a play?
11 buy one or borrow one?
12 leave today or tomorrow?
13 ask Tom or ask Jack?
14 earn money or spend it?
15 see the film first or read the book first?
16 wash them at home or take them to the launderette?
17 explain it in French or English?
18 queue for a bus or look for a taxi?
19 drive or be driven?
20 live 35 floors up or nearer the ground?

100 Expressions of preference: **I would rather you** + past tense and **I would prefer you** + infinitive

☑ PEG 297

A: Can I go by air? (train)
(a) B: *I'd rather you went by train.*
(b) B: *I'd prefer you to go by train.*

1 Can I buy a big dog? (small dog)
2 Shall I phone you when you're away? (write to me)
3 Can I study sociology at the university? (mathematics)
4 Shall I toss the pancake? (turn it with a knife)
5 Shall I put the money under my mattress? (put it in the bank)
6 Can I hang the washing out of the window? (hang it on the line)
7 Can we speak French at meals? (English)
8 Can I pay by cheque? (pay cash)
9 Can I settle the account tomorrow? (today)
10 Can I climb alone? (with a guide)
11 Shall I leave the key in the lock? (under the mat)
12 Shall I adjust the brakes myself? (ask the garage to do it)
13 Can I join the demonstration? (stay at home)
14 Shall I complain to the manager? (say nothing)
15 Shall I let the phone ring? (answer it)
16 Shall I leave the light on? (turn it off)
17 Can I wear jeans to Ann's party? (a suit)
18 Shall I cut my own hair? (go to a hairdresser)
19 Can I drive fast? (slowly)
20 Shall I send it by ordinary post? (register it)

Key

Drill 1 (a) All answers begin with *Yes*, . . .
1. we are 2. I did 3. he can 4. he has 5. she will 6. I could
7. they were 8. he did 9. he would 10. I must 11. he is
12. they were 13. they had 14. he is 15. he does
16. I have 17. he was 18. he did 19. she will 20. I must

(b) All answers begin with *No*, . . .
1. we aren't 2. I didn't 3. he can't 4. he hasn't 5. she won't
6. I couldn't 7. they weren't 8. he didn't 9. he wouldn't
10. I needn't 11. he isn't 12. they weren't 13. they hadn't
14. he isn't 15. he doesn't 16. I haven't 17. he wasn't
18. he didn't 19. she won't 20. I needn't

Drill 2 All answers have the form *I . . . but Tom . . .* , so only the
two verbs will be given in each case.
(a) 1. have, hasn't 2. did, didn't 3. do, doesn't 4. am, isn't
5. have, hasn't 6. am, isn't 7. will, won't 8. was, wasn't
9. would, wouldn't 10. must, needn't 11. can, can't 12. do,
doesn't 13. am, isn't 14. must, needn't 15. could, couldn't
16. should, shouldn't 17. had, hadn't 18. would, wouldn't 19. am,
isn't 20. have, hasn't

(b) 1. haven't, has 2. didn't, did 3. don't, does 4. I'm not, is
5. haven't, has 6. I'm not, is 7. won't, will 8. wasn't, was
9. wouldn't, would 10. needn't, must 11. can't, can 12. don't,
does 13. I'm not, is 14. needn't, must 15. couldn't, could
16. shouldn't, should 17. hadn't, had 18. wouldn't, would 19. I'm
not, is 20. haven't, has

Drill 3 (a) All answers begin with *Neither* . . .
1. has Bill 2. must Arthur 3. did his mother 4. do I 5. would her
husband 6. does James 7. has Bob 8. was Peter 9. do I 10. will
Lucy 11. am I 12. was Jack 13. should Paul 14. will she
15. had his sister 16. are the Joneses 17. can anyone else 18. has
Harold 19. could Alice 20. had Peter

(b) As above, but first repeat the original statement.

Drill 4 All answers begin with *And so* . . .
1. did/had I 2. does/has Gerald 3. has Alan 4. should we 5. did
Alice 6. is Michael 7. does he 8. did I 9. should Jane 10. will
Pat 11. did we 12. had Mark 13. are we 14. did you 15. must

his wife   16. did Mary   17. did Jean   18. should Peter   19. has
Philip   20. are we all

Drill 5   All answers repeat the prompt, followed by *but . . .*
1. Tom does   2. Peter is   3. George would   4. his wife had   5. her
sister will   6. Bob did   7. Mrs Jones has   8. your friend must
9. I could   10. we were   11. I had   12. I would   13. I can
14. we have   15. Michael does   16. their mother should
17. she had   18. Andrew would   19. Alice did   20. the conductor was

Drill 6   All answers repeat the prompt, followed by *but . . .*
1. Paul didn't   2. Paul hadn't   3. I wasn't   4. we hadn't   5. you
haven't   6. I didn't   7. I wasn't   8. his brother can't   9. I
couldn't   10. I don't   11. I wouldn't   12. the boys weren't   13. the
boys didn't   14. she doesn't   15. hers isn't   16. his father didn't
17. his sister hasn't   18. Bob needn't   19. his mother wouldn't
20. Jack doesn't

Drill 7
1. Do you?   2. Did you?   3. Was it?   4. Were they?   5. Have
you?   6. Had you?   7. Do you?   8. Does he?   9. Do you?   10. Did
you?   11. Must you?   12. Do they?   13. Is it?   14. Do you?
15. Have I?   16. Did he?   17. Would you?   18. Have you?
19. Have we?   20. Was it?

Drill 8
1. Don't you?   2. Couldn't you?   3. Weren't you?   4. Can't you?
5. Doesn't she?   6. Didn't you?   7. Haven't you?   8. Don't you?
9. Can't it?   10. Shouldn't you?   11. Don't you?   12. Didn't
you?   13. Didn't they?   14. Wasn't it?   15. Aren't I?   16. Wouldn't
you?   17. Weren't you?   18. Didn't they?   19. Don't you?
20. Wouldn't you?

Drill 9   All answers begin with *Oh, . . .*
1. you did, did you?   2. you would, would you?   3. I can, can I?   4. it
is, is it?   5. I do, do I?   6. I am, am I?   7. I will, will I?   8. you were,
were you?   9. they did, did they?   10. you do, do you?   11. they are,
are they?   12. you have, have you?   13. you did, did you?   14. you
do, do you?   15. he does, does he?   16. you are, are you?   17. you
would, would you?   18. I could, could I?   19. I am, am I?   20. they
are, are they?

Drill 10   All answers begin with *Oh, . . .*
1. you don't, don't you?   2. you aren't, aren't you?   3. you won't,
won't you?   4. they haven't, haven't they?   5. they aren't, aren't
they?   6. she doesn't, doesn't she?   7. she can't, can't she?

Key

8. I don't, don't I?   9. it wouldn't, wouldn't it?   10. I mustn't, mustn't I?   11. you aren't, aren't you?   12. I couldn't, couldn't I? 13. I wouldn't, wouldn't I?   14. he doesn't, doesn't he?   15. he didn't, didn't he?   16. he couldn't, couldn't he?   17. I shouldn't, shouldn't I?   18. you didn't, didn't you?   19. you weren't, weren't you? 20. I wasn't, wasn't I?

Drill 11   In each case repeat the statement and add the tag given below.
(a)   1. need you?   2. were they?   3. are you?   4. had they? 5. should he?   6. does she?   7. did they?   8. shall we?   9. does he?   10. do you?   11. is it?   12. could you?   13. would he?   14. will you?   15. can you?

(b)   1. haven't they?   2. aren't they?   3. won't he?   4. wasn't he?   5. didn't he?   6. shouldn't he?   7. wouldn't she?   8. don't they?   9. hadn't she?   10. isn't it?   11. don't you?   12. doesn't he?   13. oughtn't he?   14. couldn't they?   15. didn't they?

Drill 12   See note to drill 11.
1. were they?   2. did they?   3. mustn't there?   4. is it?   5. won't you?   6. had they?   7. shouldn't they?   8. would there?   9. aren't I?   10. hadn't we?   11. did you?   12. wasn't he?   13. won't it? 14. will he?   15. wouldn't he?   16. can't you?   17. do you? 18. am I?   19. are you?   20. mightn't we?

Drill 13   See note to drill 11.
1. didn't he?   2. has she?   3. won't it?   4. couldn't they?   5. do you?   6. will they?   7. wasn't it?   8. used he?/did he?   9. are you?   10. would he?   11. didn't you?   12. hadn't we?   13. are they?   14. can't it?   15. are we?   16. do they?   17. didn't they?   18. shouldn't it?   19. need it?   20. wouldn't you?

Drill 14   All answers have the form *I can . . . but I can't . . .*

Drill 15   All the answers begin with *No, . . .*
1. I had it painted   2. I have it cut   3. I'm going to have it mended 4. he has it washed   5. she has them polished   6. I'm going to have them shortened   7. I have them typed   8. I'd have them adjusted 9. I'm having them dyed   10. I had it towed   11. I'm going to have it cut down   12. I had it repaired   13. I have them sharpened   14. he has it tuned   15. she has them swept   16. he's having them taught   17. he had it built   18. he had them planted   19. she's having it translated   20. she's having it made

Drill 16 All answers begin with *No, . . .*
1. she shortened it herself   2. she cleans them herself   3. he's going
to re-spray it himself   4. he checks them himself   5. I whitewashed it
myself   6. he drew it up himself   7. I put it up myself   8. he mends
them himself   9. I'm planting them myself   10. I'm going to pick them
myself   11. she sweeps them herself   12. she takes them
herself   13. I clean them myself   14. I checked them myself   15. she
sets it herself   16. he delivered them himself   17. she frames them
herself   18. he's developing it himself   19. he cut it down
himself   20. he took it out himself

Drill 17 Any logical answer is acceptable. The following are
suggested answers only.
1. and had to wait for the second   2. so we had to stand   3. so we had
to carry our own luggage   4. so I had to go to the booking-office
5. and had to buy another one   6. so I had to sleep in my car   7. and
had to ask   8. so I had to pay by cheque   9. so I had to look it up
10. I had to ring the bell   11. so I had to phone from a call-box
12. we had to use the stairs   13. and had to change the wheel   14. so
we had to finish our meal by candle-light   15. and had to ask Tom to
explain it   16. I had to renew it   17. and had to buy food outside
18. and had to ask him to repeat it   19. so we had to turn back   20. so
I had to call the Fire Brigade

Drill 18 Each answer has the form *Oh we didn't have to* + infinitive +
phrase given. It is therefore only necessary to give the infinitives.
1. wear   2. talk   3. get up   4. wash   5. run   6. be   7. learn
8. clean   9. make   10. look   11. keep   12. serve   13. eat
14. help   15. work   16. write   17. let   18. ask   19. do   20. play

Drill 19 Each answer has the form *Then you'd better . . . today*.
1. do it   2. apologize   3. explain   4. apply   5. enrol   6. finish it
7. wash it   8. mend it   9. fix it   10. pay it   11. return them
12. decide   13. suggest it   14. book them   15. order it
16. advertise it   17. answer it   18. report it   19. renew it   20. see
him about it

Drill 20 Each answer has the form, *Yes, but . . . tomorrow*.
1. she's to look after Jack's children   2. they are to work with Jack's
group   3. I'm to follow Jack   4. I'm to drive Jack's car   5. she's to
lead Jack's team   6. he's to ride Jack's horse   7. I'm to relieve
Jack   8. I'm to act as lookout for Jack   9. they're to take their orders
from Jack   10. I'm to train with Jack   11. I'm to stand in front of
Jack   12. They're to test Jack   13. she's to film Jack's group   14. I'm
to navigate for Jack   15. We're to give Jack a lift

Key

Drill 21 All answers have the form *I was to . . . at 6.00.*
1. report 2. post them 3. meet him 4. contact her 5. see
them 6. collect it 7. relieve him 8. join 9. leave 10. pay
them 11. release them 12. inspect it 13. take off 14. start
15. open them

Drill 22 All answers have the form *No, we were to have . . . but the
plan fell through.*
1. camped on the beach 2. hired a boat 3. visited the island
4. anchored in the bay 5. explored the caves 6. bathed by
moonlight 7. spent a week there 8. collected driftwood 9. cooked
over open fires 10. made a film of the seabirds 11. swum before
breakfast 12. water-skied 13. kept a temperature chart 14. got up
at dawn 15. recorded the dawn chorus 16. climbed the cliffs
17. searched for the sunken treasure-ship 18. taken photographs
under water 19. had sing-songs round the camp fire 20. invited
everyone to a barbecue

Drill 23 Each question has two answers. These will be given
together. The first answer has the form: *Well he/she/they may have . . . ,
I suppose.* The second answer has the form: *I said he/she/they might
have . . .* For each question, therefore, we will give only the subject
and the past participle + the rest of the sentence.
1. he, stolen it 2. she, sold it 3. you, lost it 4. she, drunk it
5. he, thrown it away 6. they, pawned it 7. she, left it at home
8. he, eaten it 9. they, hidden it in the attic 10. he, burnt it
11. she, torn it up 12. she, forgotten to claim it 13. they had an
accident 14. it, broken down 15. he, advised them not to
come 16. he, fallen overboard 17. they, got lost 18. he, been
murdered 19. something, delayed them 20. he, taken the wrong
drug

Drill 24 No answers are given as for each (a) answer the student
merely has to replace *am is/are* by *may be.* For each (b) answer the
student merely has to replace *was/were* by *may have been.* (*might* can be
used instead of *may* throughout.)

Drill 25 Each answer has the form *You should have . . . at once.*
1. asked him 2. paid it 3. thanked him 4. looked for it 5. invited
him 6. apologized 7. sent it back 8. returned 9. reported it
10. booked them 11. answered it 12. cooked it 13. written to
him 14. rung him up 15. started 16. begun 17. eaten it
18. spoken to him 19. given it to him 20. complained

106

Drill 26   Each answer has the form *You shouldn't have . . . anyone.*
1. asked   2. invited   3. reported   4. paid   5. fined   6. sacked
7. complained about   8. argued with   9. played   10. discussed it
with   11. talked about it with   12. woken   13. written to
14. shouted at   15. thrown stones at   16. told lies to
17. robbed   18. cheated   19. winked at   20. kissed

Drill 27   Each answer has the form *No. Should I have . . .*
1. read them   2. tried to stop her   3. listened to it   4. tipped him
5. followed them   6. kept it   7. threatened him   8. stood up
9. refused   10. offered to help   11. made her wear it   12. put it
up   13. taken it down   14. worn them   15. brought it   16. notified
them   17. locked them up   18. burnt them   19. given it back
20. rung it

Drill 28   Each answer has the form *he/she/they shouldn't be . . . now.*
He/she/they should have . . . before etc.
1. she . . . doing them . . . done them   2. he . . . correcting
them . . . corrected them   3. he . . . polishing them . . . polished
them   4. he . . . tying them . . . tied them   5. she . . . putting them
on . . . put them on   6. she . . . sewing it on . . . sewn it on
7. he . . . eating it . . . eaten it   8. she . . . putting it on . . . put it
on   9. he . . . brushing it . . . brushed it   10. he . . . putting them
in . . . put them in   11. he . . . filing them . . . filed them
12. he . . . combing it . . . combed it   13. she . . . cleaning them . . .
cleaned them   14. they . . . doing it . . . done it
15. he . . . putting them in . . . put them in

Drill 29   (a) Each answer has the form *She shouldn't be . . . she should
be . . .*
1. getting up . . . having breakfast   2. having breakfast . . . washing
up   3. washing up . . . doing PT   4. doing PT . . . watching the
television programme   5. watching television . . . discussing the
programme   6. listening to a lecture . . . helping with the lunch
7. playing tennis . . . resting   8. resting . . . working in the
garden   9. working in the garden . . . playing tennis   10. having
tea . . . practising the piano   11. practising the piano . . . rehearsing
the play   12. rehearsing the play . . . having supper   13. having
supper . . . typing her notes   14. typing her notes . . . reading in the
library   15. listening to records . . . sleeping/asleep/in bed.

(b) Answers as above, but with *Shouldn't have been . . . should have
been*

Key

Drill 30   Each answer begins *Peter must have* . . .
1. borrowed it   2. washed up   3. left them   4. dropped it
5. polished it   6. swept them   7. made them   8. bolted it   9. paid
it   10. ordered it   11. eaten them   12. drunk it   13. reported
it   14. had a party   15. driven into a wall   16. wound it   17. cut
himself   18. left the tap on   19. taken them down   20. put it up

Drill 31   Each answer has the form *Tom couldn't have* . . . *he wasn't
here yesterday.*
1. spoken to her   2. paid him   3. brought them   4. fixed it   5. tuned
it   6. made it   7. moved it   8. split it   9. opened them
10. borrowed it   11. answered it   12. finished it   13. drunk it
14. eaten it   15. fused them   16. left it on   17. let them out
18. overheard us   19. planted them   20. gone off with it

Drill 32   Each answer has the form *He couldn't have* + past participle
+ rest of sentence.
1. had   2. bolted   3. used   4. come   5. slept   6. bought
7. hired   8. driven   9. taken   10. carried   11. dined
12. waded   13. watched   14. seen   15. been   16. walked
17. got   18. swum   19. heard   20. gone

Drill 33   Each answer has the form (1) *No, I* . . . (2) *You needn't
have* . . . *You could have* . . .
1. took a bus. taken a bus . . . gone by taxi.   2. walked. walked . . .
gone by bus.   3. walked up the stairs. walked up the stairs . . . taken
the lift.   4. wrote. written . . . phoned.   5. stood in a queue. stood in
a queue . . . got the tickets from a machine.   6. bought them. bought
them . . . borrowed them.   7. carried them. carried them . . . asked
the shop to send them.   8. had it sprayed. had it sprayed . . . painted
it yourself.   9. used the machine. used the machine . . . sewed it by
hand.   10. took the ski-lift. taken the ski-lift . . . walked up the ski-
slope.   11. paid cash. paid cash . . . by cheque.   12. asked the
exchange to get. asked the exchange to get . . . dialled direct.
13. sent for the electrician. sent for the electrician . . . replaced it
yourself.   14. rang for the Fire Brigade. rung for the Fire Brigade . . .
put it out yourself.   15. moved it out of the room. moved it out of the
room . . . covered it with a sheet.   16. threw the coat away. thrown
the coat away . . . sewn the button on.   17. went first class. gone first
class . . . gone second class.   18. sat in the dark. sat in the dark . . .
put in a new fuse.   19. took it with me. taken it with you . . . left it at
the station.   20. typed it twice. typed it twice . . . used a carbon.

Drill 34   All answers have the form *But you needn't have had . . . you could have . . . yourself.*
1. it painted . . . painted it   2. them dyed . . . dyed them   3. it cleaned . . . cleaned it · 4. it cut down . . . cut it down   5. it put in . . . put it in   6. it installed . . . installed it   7. it repaired . . . repaired it   8. it mended . . . mended it   9. them pruned . . . pruned them   10. them washed . . . washed them   11. it resprayed . . . resprayed it   12. it repapered . . . repapered it   13. them planted . . . planted them   14. it built . . . built it   15. it made . . . made it   16. it framed . . . framed it   17. it polished . . . polished it   18. it fitted . . . fitted it   19. them picked . . . picked them   20. it tuned . . . tuned it

Drill 35   Each answer has the form *Couldn't . . . have . . . before?*
1. you . . . posted it   2. they . . . paid you   3. she . . . started   4. he . . . brought it back   5. he . . . sent it in   6. you . . . phoned him   7. they . . . moved out   8. you . . . left   9. she . . . written   10. he . . . applied   11. he . . . booked them   12. they . . . reported it   13. you . . . re-addressed them   14. you . . . got back   15. you . . . made them   16. you . . . cancelled them   17. you . . . answered it   18. you . . . given it to her   19. you . . . invited him   20. you . . . told them about it

Drill 36   Each answer has the form *No, he/she . . . his/her own +* object.
1. he irons his   2. he washes his   3. she makes her   4. he ties his   5. he brushes his   6. he chooses his   7. he sews on his   8. he cleans his   9. he gets his   10. she does her   11. he cooks his   12. she polishes her   13. he checks his   14. he pumps up his   15. he does his   16. he cleans his   17. she cuts her   18. he gets his   19. he types his   20. he pays his

Drill 37   Each answer has the form *Tom* + verb + phrase as in pattern. Verbs only will be given.
1. works   2. lives   3. gets up   4. goes   5. has   6. runs   7. comes   8. catches   9. gets   10. reads   11. gets out   12. starts   13. lunches   14. finishes   15. goes   16. stands   17. sits   18. buys   19. arrives   20. says

Drill 38   Each answer consists of a statement followed by a question. The questions are merely repetitions of the question asked by A, with *you* stressed. The statements are given below. Each answer begins with *Yes, I . . .*
1. eat in the canteen   2. start at nine   3. finish at six   4. weigh ten stone   5. am six foot tall   6. get up at seven   7. like dogs best

Key

8. come by bus   9. watch TV   10. go to Scotland   11. have three
weeks   12. keep it under the mattress   13. buy them in Paris
14. do it just before the lesson   15. write home every week   16. like
it strong   17. cook on gas   18. play tennis best   19. swim in the
swimming baths   20. drink gin

Drill 39   This is an open-ended exercise. The following are possible
answers only. They all begin: *Tom* . . .
1. smokes cigarettes   2. lives on the ground floor   3. spends a lot
4. goes by bus   5. spends Saturdays at home   6. travels by train
7. writes with his right hand   8. eats with a fork   9. drinks water
10. watches tennis   11. stays at home   12. employs an electrician
13. sleeps with the windows shut   14. writes his own letters
15. types his (essays)   16. speaks French   17. agrees with him
18. thinks it is essential   19. wears his hair long   20. makes very
few mistakes

Drill 40   Each answer has the form . . . *does your brother* . . . ?
1. Where . . . live?   2. How many . . . smoke?   3. What . . .
have?   4. What . . . read?   5. Where . . . go?   6. How much . . .
spend?   7. What . . . drive?   8. What . . . wear?   9. How many . . .
employ?   10. Where . . . bank?   11. How . . . pay?   12. What . . .
like best?   13. When . . . clean his flat?   14. Where . . . keep his
bicycle?   15. What . . . sing?   16. What . . . play?   17. How
often . . . phone?   18. Where . . . sit?   19. What . . . collect?
20. What . . . write?

Drill 41   In each answer the word *usually* is placed between *don't/
doesn't* and the infinitive.
1. doesn't . . . answer the telephone   2. doesn't . . . take the children
to school   3. doesn't . . . help his wife   4. doesn't . . . look after the
baby   5. doesn't . . . walk the dog   6. doesn't . . . carry his wife's
basket   7. doesn't . . . clean the windows   8. doesn't . . . mow the
lawn   9. doesn't . . . weed the garden   10. doesn't . . . hang out the
washing   11. don't . . . spend their holidays at home   12. don't . . .
do crossword puzzles   13. don't . . . work late   14. don't . . . knock
off early   15. doesn't . . . cook it in butter   16. doesn't . . . bake
bread   17. doesn't . . . look miserable   18. doesn't . . . sleep on my
bed   19. doesn't . . . drive her husband's car   20. doesn't . . . stop
at the traffic lights

Drill 42   Each answer has the form *isn't/doesn't his sister* + verb +
the rest of the original sentence + *as well.*
1. doesn't . . . go   2. doesn't . . . drive   3. doesn't . . . live
4. isn't . . . learning   5. doesn't . . . lose   6. isn't . . . planning

7. doesn't . . . drink   8. doesn't . . . give   9. doesn't . . . know
10. doesn't . . . play   11. doesn't . . . employ   12. isn't . . .
building   13. isn't . . . buying   14. doesn't . . . collect   15. isn't . . .
starting   16. doesn't . . . spend   17. doesn't . . . eat   18. isn't . . .
terrified   19. isn't . . . always grumbling   20. isn't . . . thinking

Drill 43   Each answer has the form *But today he is* + . . . *French* . . .
1. driving a   2. riding a   3. singing   4. playing   5. drinking
6. dancing with a   7. using a   8. having lunch in a   9. listening to the
news in   10. writing in   11. going to a   12. talking   13. correcting
the   14. explaining in   15. lecturing in   16. broadcasting in
17. addressing students in   18. cooking a   19. travelling by a
20. swearing in

Drill 44   Each answer has the form *doesn't* + subject + *usually* +
infinitive + rest of sentence.
1. he . . . go   2. she . . . smoke   3. she . . . do   4. she . . .
wear   5. he . . . wash   6. he . . . buy   7. he . . . tell   8. he . . .
have   9. he . . . cook   10. he . . . make   11. he . . . type
12. he . . . stand   13. he . . . sit   14. he . . . dance   15. she . . .
play   16. he . . . listen   17. she . . . go   18. it . . . make
19. he . . . go on strike   20. he . . . get

Drill 45   Each answer has the form *Then why is/are* + subject + . . .
+ rest of sentence + *today.*
1. is he grumbling   2. are they complaining   3. is he swearing   4. are
they paying   5. is he writing   6. is he walking   7. is he lunching
8. is she standing   9. is he sitting   10. is he using   11. is she
criticizing   12. is he making   13. is she bringing   14. is he
smiling   15. are they leaving   16. is he locking   17. is he typing
18. is he emptying   19. is he taking   20. is he watching

Drill 46   In each case the first answer has the form *Oh, are you
thinking of* . . . + rest of sentence. The second answer has the form *I
asked if you were thinking of* . . .
1. selling   2. leaving   3. giving up your   4. asking Jack
5. emigrating   6. buying   7. hiring   8. sleeping   9. going
10. sending   11. having   12. complaining   13. threatening
14. offering   15. robbing   16. painting   17. hitch-hiking
18. reporting   19. applying   20. throwing

Drill 47   This is a free exercise.

Drill 48   Follow the pattern closely and there should be no problem.

Key

Drill 49   Each answer begins with *No, . . .*
1. we didn't start till nine   2. we didn't arrive till the fourth   3. it doesn't begin till ten   4. they don't shut till six   5. he doesn't get up till eight   6. we aren't going till Thursday   7. he didn't call us till seven   8. he isn't leaving till Saturday   9. he didn't pay us till the end of the second week   10. he didn't get there till the 25th   11. they aren't coming till August   12. I don't expect to be ready till May   13. it's not being produced till June   14. it doesn't come till nine   15. I'm not starting (it) till next week   16. I'm not seeing him till Friday   17. they didn't report it till the second   18. he wasn't arrested till the next day   19. they didn't operate till the fifth   20. they aren't releasing him till tomorrow

Drill 50   (a) Each answer has the form *Oh yes, he does. He's always . . .* (b) Each answer has the form *Oh yes, he did. He was always . . .* The rest of the answer is the same in each case.
1. smoking   2. asking for help   3. talking about her   4. arguing   5. forgetting my telephone number   6. using the phone   7. changing his job   8. having accidents   9. getting into trouble   10. gossiping   11. boasting   12. breaking things   13. looking out of the window   14. letting me down   15. grumbling   16. telling lies   17. getting into debt   18. catching cold   19. writing to the newspapers   20. ordering me about

Drill 51   Each answer has the form *Nonsense! He only . . . twice!*
1. interrupted   2. complained   3. interfered   4. changed his mind   5. lost his temper   6. got drunk   7. broke his promise   8. fell off   9. woke you up   10. disappeared   11. went on strike   12. made a fuss   13. refused   14. came late   15. asked for a rise   16. shouted at you   17. left work early   18. took her out   19. got lost   20. overslept

Drill 52   For the first answers put the verb in the prompt into the past continuous tense, first person e.g. *I was listening to the radio.* For the second answers replace *I was* by *I went on.*

Drills 53, 54, 55, 56 are pronunciation exercises with regular verbs.

Drill 57   Each answer has the form *Yes, but today I . . .*
1. got out at Piccadilly   2. drank wine   3. met him at his club   4. felt awful   5. read *The Times*   6. sent them by hand   7. told Janet first   8. went with Paul   9. came by taxi   10. said too much   11. bought pears   12. stood at the back   13. sat upstairs   14. left at

nine   15. wrote three pages   16. put it in the drawer   17. rang her at
six   18. woke them at seven   19. spent hardly anything   20. made a
loss

Drill 58   Each answer has the form *Yes . . . yesterday.*
1. I sold it   2. I spoke to him   3. I lost it   4. they heard it   5. they
drank it   6. I rang him   7. she saw it   8. I paid it   9. I caught
one   10. he broke it off   11. I learnt them   12. he tore them   13. he
forgot   14. she began   15. I found them   16. I burnt them   17. she
swept them   18. I threw it away   19. I gave it to him   20. I ground it

Drill 59   Each answer begins *When did you last . . .*
1. drink it   2. speak it   3. read one   4. tell one   5. break one
6. write to him   7. have one   8. make one   9. fly   10. drive
one   11. ride it   12. get lost   13. buy something   14. cut it
15. keep him waiting   16. miss one   17. pay it   18. sleep well
19. quarrel with him   20. hear from her

Drill 60   Each answer has the form *Didn't you . . . Jack too?*
1. help   2. thank   3. pay   4. congratulate   5. fine   6. speak to
7. meet   8. write to   9. see   10. tip   11. photograph   12. send a
card to   13. get a ticket for   14. keep a seat for   15. ask
16. invite   17. forgive   18. offer a lift to   19. stop   20. warn

Drill 61   Each answer begins *I thought . . .*
1. you drank tea   2. he smoked a pipe   3. you left (home) at 9.00
4. you started (work) at 10.00   5. you ate in a restaurant
6. you got up at 7.00   7. you made £50 a week   8. he wrote love
stories   9. it left at 4.30   10. you spent £2 (a week)   11. you came
from Wales   12. you played golf   13. you collected stamps   14. you
agreed with Paul   15. you always had lunch with George   16. you
painted in oils   17. you needed a chisel   18. he preferred Mary
19. you cooked it in oil   20. he sold radios

Drill 62   (a) Each answer has the form *I thought you . . . Pimlico.*
1. worked in   2. shopped in   3. lived in   4. went to classes in   5. left
your car in   6. met in   7. sent his mail to   8. got out at   9. caught
your train at   10. bought your shoes in   11. played tennis in
12. preferred   13. wanted a garage in   14. spent your weekends
in   15. he refused to live in

(b) Each answer has the form *Oh, I thought you . . . French.*
1. spoke   2. corrected his   3. sang in   4. wrote the minutes of the
meeting in   5. complained in   6. argued in   7. tested their

Key

8. shouted at him   9. translated them into   10. gave the instructions
in   11. explained in   12. swore in   13. thought in   14. counted in
15. discussed it in

Drill 63   Each answer begins *I didn't know* . . .
1. you knitted   2. she skated   3. he boxed   4. she fished   5. he
fenced   6. she painted   7. he water-skied   8. he dived   9. you
sailed   10. she gardened   11. he played football   12. he smoked
cigars   13. they rode motorbikes   14. you collected stamps   15. you
flew helicopters   16. you wore contact lenses   17. he climbed
18. you made speeches   19. you led demonstrations   20. you told
fortunes

Drill 64   Each answer has the form *No* + subject + *has/have only
just* . . .
1. I've . . . heard it   2. he's . . . arrived   3. she's . . . left
4. they've . . . got engaged   5. she's . . . arranged it   6. she's . . .
accepted it   7. they've . . . bought it   8. he's . . . told her
9. it's . . . begun   10. it's . . . opened   11. he's . . . suggested
it   12. we've . . . enrolled   13. he's . . . passed it   14. I've . . .
signed it   15. they've . . . cancelled it   16. he's . . . resigned
17. they've . . . emigrated   18. they've . . . arrested him
19. he's . . . answered   20. I've . . . booked them

Drill 65   Each answer begins *How* . . .
1. many have you planted?   2. many have you made?   3. many has he
cleaned?   4. many has he written?   5. many have you mended?
6. many have you washed?   7. many have you applied for?   8. many
have you taken?   9. much have you saved?   10. much has he put
on?   11. much has she lost?   12. many has he answered?   13. many
has she sent?   14. many have you cut?   15. many has he
painted?   16. many has he looked at?   17. many have you
addressed?   18. many have you ironed?   19. much have you
ground?   20. many have you peeled?

Drill 66   Each answer begins *Oh* and ends: *for ages.*
1. I haven't seen him   2. I haven't made one   3. we haven't eaten
out   4. he hasn't done one   5. I haven't slept well   6. she hasn't read
one   7. he hasn't taken part in one   8. I haven't heard from them
9. I haven't flown one   10. I haven't spoken to him   11. he hasn't
taught   12. he hasn't paid me   13. he hasn't written (to me)
14. I haven't been (to the theatre)   15. I haven't caught one
16. he hasn't shaved   17. he hasn't had one   18. I haven't sold one
19. we haven't discussed it   20. I haven't won one

Drill 67   Each answer begins *How long . . .*
1. have you been working here?   2. have you been learning Greek?
3. have you been waiting for Peter?   4. have you been sleeping
badly?   5. have you been economizing?   6. has he been driving a
bus?   7. have you been checking their accounts?   8. have you been
paying his school fees?   9. has he been cooking?   10. has she been
doing two jobs?   11. have you been feeling depressed?   12. has he
been blackmailing you?   13. has he been sending anonymous letters?
14. have you been collecting fossils?   15. has he been receiving stolen
goods?   16. have they been meeting secretly?   17. have you been
losing weight?   18. have you been helping Peter with his
homework?   19. have you been living in a condemned house?
20. have they been squatting in the empty block?

Drill 68   Each answer has the form *No, when I arrived he'd just . . .*
1. posted it   2. resigned   3. accepted them   4. rung her   5. signed
it   6. confessed   7. admitted it   8. refused it   9. left   10. taken
them   11. bought them   12. sold it   13. cancelled it   14. told
him   15. showed it to them   16. proposed to her   17. started
18. cut it down   19. burnt them   20. shot her

Drill 69   For each answer replace the first eight words of the question
(*When . . . started*) by *No, he'd been*, add the rest of the question and
then add *for some time* e.g. 1. *No, he'd been* receiving stolen goods *for
some time.*

Drill 70   (a) Each answer has the form *Yes, we're . . . on Tuesday.*
(b) As above, except that each answer begins: *He said they were . . .*
1. leaving   2. starting   3. setting off   4. moving out   5. coming
back   6. returning   7. demonstrating   8. marching   9. taking it
10. announcing it   11. interviewing them   12. testing it   13. opening
it   14. launching it   15. meeting him   16. inspecting them
17. inviting them   18. seeing him   19. hiring it   20. making it

Drill 71   (a) Each answer will begin *I'll . . .*
1. tell the Principal   2. send out invitations   3. put up notices
4. sweep the floor   5. wash the windows   6. lay the tables   7. hire
the glasses   8. cut sandwiches   9. order the wine   10. open the
bottles   11. make the coffee   12. bring milk and sugar   13. hire a
disc jockey   14. look after guests' coats   15. supervise the
parking   16. borrow records   17. keep the accounts   18. take back
the empties   19. wash up the dirty dishes   20. tip the caretaker

(b) 1. Tom's telling him   2. Ann's sending them out   3. Jack's putting
them up   4. Mary's sweeping it   5. Alec's cleaning them   6. Bill's
laying them   7. Joan's hiring them   8. Alice's cutting them

9. Peter's ordering it   10. Bill's opening them   11. Hilda's making
it   12. Vera's bringing them   13. Andrew's hiring him   14. Hugh's
looking after them   15. George's supervising it   16. Jill's borrowing
them   17. Michael's keeping them   18. Rupert's taking them
back   19. Brian's washing them up   20. John's tipping him

Drill 72   (a) Each answer has the form *I'm afraid I forgot! But I'll . . .*
tomorrow. (b) Each answer has the form *No, she forgot, but she said*
she'd . . . tomorrow. Otherwise the answers are identical.
1. tell him   2. ring her   3. ask him   4. remind him   5. pay him
6. thank her   7. help them   8. book them   9. get it   10. answer it
11. sweep them   12. apologize to him   13. invite them   14. burn it
15. wind it   16. take them back   17. buy them   18. make it
19. check them   20. insure it

Drill 73   Each answer has the form *No, I'm going to . . .*
1. apply for it   2. tell them   3. complain about it   4. report him
5. buy one   6. hire one   7. record it   8. pay it   9. raise it
10. employ her   11. warn them   12. write to him   13. repair it
14. invite them   15. send him   16. sell it   17. accept it   18. have it
at home   19. build one   20. let it

Drill 74   Each answer has the form *Yes, but I'm not going to . . .*
tomorrow.
1. get up first   2. grind it   3. make it   4. wash up   5. leave it at
home   6. let you drive   7. ring you   8. come straight home   9. bring
you flowers   10. do it for you   11. bath him   12. play with them
13. repair it   14. blow it up   15. read to them   16. mow it
17. water them   18. help you wash up   19. invite her round
20. babysit

Drill 75   Each answer has the form *He/she/they hasn't/haven't said*
anything but I suppose . . .
1. they haven't . . . they'll invite her   2. he hasn't . . . he'll pay for
it   3. he hasn't . . . he'll apply for it   4. he hasn't . . . he'll have it
5. they haven't . . . they'll sell it   6. they haven't . . . they'll let it
7. he hasn't . . . he'll resign   8. they haven't . . . they'll take on more
staff   9. she hasn't . . . she'll fly   10. they haven't . . . they'll re-
enrol   11. he hasn't . . . he'll go abroad   12. he hasn't . . . he'll enter
for it   13. they haven't . . . they'll speak   14. he hasn't . . . he'll
play   15. they haven't . . . they'll stay for some time
16. he hasn't . . . he'll come back   17. she hasn't . . . she'll go on
with it   18. they haven't . . . they'll get married soon   19. he
hasn't . . . he'll take her with him   20. they haven't . . . they'll
celebrate it

Drill 76   In each case replace *Paul's on holiday he's* by *This time next week I'll,* add the rest of the question and *too,* e.g. *This time next week I'll* be sunbathing *too.*

Drill 77   Each answer begins *Will you be* . . .
1. letting it next August   2. lunching with him next Monday
3. leaving early next Friday   4. going camping next summer
5. having a drink with him next Tuesday   6. giving her a lift home next Wednesday   7. playing golf next Sunday   8. ringing him next Saturday   9. taking her out next Monday   10. sailing next Saturday   11. watching (television) next Sunday evening   12. taking them for a walk next week-end   13. listening to it next Sunday morning   14. writing to him next Thursday   15. typing them next Friday   16. doing them next Saturday   17. changing it next Thursday   18. meeting him next Tuesday   19. dining out next Friday   20. visiting her next Wednesday

Drill 78   Each answer has the form *She won't be* . . . *tomorrow; she's just been given the day off.*
1. opening the mail   2. dusting the boss's desk   3. answering the phone   4. doing the translating   5. dealing with dissatisfied customers   6. receiving new clients   7. taking shorthand notes
8. writing the minutes   9. typing the reports   10. filing the copies   11. making the tea   12. bringing the tea round
13. addressing the letters   14. arranging the boss's interviews
15. checking the petty cash   16. programming the computer
17. paying the staff   18. working out the tax   19. operating the photo-copier   20. turning out the lights

Drill 79   (a) Each answer begins *Oh, she'll be* . . .
1. dressing the baby   2. cooking breakfast   3. having breakfast
4. taking the children to school   5. doing housework   6. reading the paper   7. shopping   8. cooking lunch   9. having lunch   10. writing letters   11. taking the dogs for a walk   12. collecting the children from school   13. giving the children their tea   14. helping the children with their homework   15. picking up her husband at the station
16. reading to the children   17. putting the baby to bed   18. cooking supper   19. having supper   20. washing up

(b) Each answer has the form *No, don't ring then. She'll be* . . .
1. dressing the baby   2. cooking breakfast   3. having breakfast
4. taking the children to school   5. shopping   6. cooking lunch
7. having lunch   8. taking the dogs for a walk   9. collecting the children from school   10. giving the children their tea   11. picking up

her husband at the station   12. putting the baby to bed   13. cooking
supper   14. having supper   15. going to bed

Drill 80   Each answer has the form *No, she'll have . . . by now.*
1. cooked it   2. had it   3. taken them   4. done it   5. written
them   6. walked them   7. collected them   8. given them their tea/
given it to them   9. helped them with their homework/helped them
with it   10. picked him up   11. read to them   12. put him to
bed   13. cooked it   14. washed up   15. gone to bed

Drill 81   Each answer has the form *No, I'll have . . . all by the end of
the week.*
1. painted them   2. changed them   3. rewired them   4. laid
them   5. washed them   6. hung them   7. repapered them
8. cleared them   9. varnished it   10. weeded them   11. mowed
it   12. patched them   13. ironed them   14. planted them   15. sown
them   16. replaced them   17. scrubbed them   18. polished it
19. picked them   20. bottled it

Drill 82   Each answer has the form *Oh no. By the end of the month I'll
have been* + participle + rest of sentence + *for five years.* e.g. *Oh no.
By the end of the month I'll have been* collecting stamps *for five years.*

Drill 83   (a) Each answer begins *Well, if I see him I'll . . .*

(b) Each answer begins *I said if I saw him I'd . . .* Otherwise (a) and
(b) answers are the same.
1. ask him   2. thank him   3. pay her   4. remind her   5. warn
them   6. tell them   7. apologize to him   8. kiss him   9. congratulate
them   10. invite her   11. discuss it with him   12. explain it to
her   13. show them to him   14. give it to her   15. recommend it to
him   16. suggest it to him   17. offer it to him   18. point it out to
him   19. speak to her   20. hand it to him

(c) Each exercise has the form *Yes I'll . . . as soon as he comes in.*
Otherwise the answers are as given for (a) and (b) above.

(d) Each answer has the form: *I said I'd . . . as soon as he came in.*
Otherwise the answers are as given for (a) and (b) above.

Drill 84   Each answer has the form *Well, if he . . . please let me know.*
1. complains   2. asks for more money   3. goes on strike
4. objects   5. makes a fuss   6. threatens you   7. demands an
explanation   8. tries to bribe you   9. accuses you   10. blames
you   11. refuses to co-operate   12. wants proof   13. reports you to
the police   14. takes your passport away   15. makes conditions

16. argues   17. insists on a written agreement   18. hi-jacks your plane   19. kidnaps you   20. shoots at you

Drill 85   Each answer has the form *But unless he . . . today he'll be too late.*
1. comes   2. begins   3. decides   4. signs   5. applies   6. leaves
7. sends it   8. posts it   9. tells us   10. sets out   11. books them   12. pays   13. claims it   14. reports it   15. arrives
16. enrols   17. goes   18. accepts   19. flies   20. arranges it

Drill 86   Each answer has the form *I'm afraid so. I'd . . . if I could but I can't.*
1. meet you   2. see you off   3. help you   4. wait for you   5. keep you a place   6. show you the way   7. fix it for you   8. translate if for you   9. give you a lift   10. carry it for you   11. find you a job   12. go with you   13. babysit   14. take over   15. do it   16. arrange it for you   17. drive you   18. explain it to you   19. show you how to do it   20. advise you

Drill 87   (*I/we should* can replace *I'd/We'd.*)
1. If I were nice and slim I'd look marvellous in tight jeans too   2. If I had plenty of money I'd spend the winters abroad too   3. If I worked overtime I'd earn a lot of money too   4. If my garden got a lot of sun I could grow peaches too   5. If I could ski I'd go skiing at Christmas too   6. If we used electric typewriters we'd finish early too   7. If I knew a film director I'd get good parts too   8. If I got two hours for lunch I'd go to lunch-time concerts too   9. If we both worked we could afford expensive holidays too   10. If I read the newspapers carefully I'd know what was happening too   11. If I ran round the park every morning I'd keep very fit too   12. If I travelled first class I'd enjoy travelling too   13. If I employed an au pair girl I could spend all day reading novels too   14. If my alarm clock rang very loudly I'd always wake up in time too   15. If my husband left the car at home I'd go shopping in it too   16. If we did our own decorating we'd save a lot of money too   17. If I belonged to a club I'd meet a lot of people too   18. If I met a lot of people I'd make a lot of friends too   19. If I had everything I wanted I'd be perfectly happy too   20. If I understood electricity I'd do my own repairs too

Drill 88   Each answer has the form *If I were on holiday I'd be +* participle + rest of sentence + *too*, e.g. *If I were on holiday now I'd be pony-trekking too.*

119

Key

Drill 89   Each answer has the form *You didn't tell me to. If you'd told me to, I'd have . . . of course.*
1. waited for him   2. met him   3. thanked him   4. warned her
5. reminded them   6. invited them   7. rung her   8. sent it
9. phoned him   10. written to him   11. reported it   12. asked
him   13. proposed him   14. sacked him   15. looked for him
16. followed him   17. searched it   18. voted for him   19. stopped
it   20. opposed it

Drill 90   Each answer has the form *Would you have . . . if he had asked you?*
1. waited for him   2. helped him   3. seen him off   4. shown them to
him   5. lent it to him   6. painted it   7. opened it   8. photographed
them   9. ironed them   10. written to him   11. explained
12. paid   13. moved it   14. done it again   15. typed it   16. given it
to him   17. changed them   18. kept it a secret   19. married him
20. contributed

Drill 91   (a) Each answer begins *So if . . .* and ends: *would you?*
1. you'd had the paper qualifications, you'd have got the post   2. you'd
done the last question, you'd have passed   3. you'd known his
number, you'd have rung him   4. you'd taken his threats seriously,
you'd have told the police   5. he'd finished the job, you'd have paid
him   6. you'd realized he was ill, you'd have given him the day off
7. your gun had been loaded, you'd have fired   8. your wife had
encouraged you, you'd have got to the top   9. they'd given you a work
permit, you'd have stayed here   10. you'd heard him knocking, you'd
have opened the door

(b) Each answer begins *So if . . .* and ends: *eh?*
1. you had known you were overdrawn, you wouldn't have given them
a cheque   2. you had been given correct information, you wouldn't
have arrived at a false conclusion   3. they had shut the loading door
properly, the plane wouldn't have crashed   4. he had loved her,
he wouldn't have deceived her   5. had known the whole story, you
wouldn't have blamed Tom   6. they had had enough lifeboats, there
wouldn't have been such a loss of life   7. he had been able to swim,
he wouldn't have been drowned   8. he had tied up the boat, it wouldn't
have drifted away   9. you had realized the lion was dangerous, you
wouldn't have opened the cage   10. you had expected him to ring back
at once, you wouldn't have gone out

Drill 92 (*Was* is replaceable by *were.*)
(a) 1. No, she isn't. I wish she was 2. No, I can't. I wish I could
3. No, I don't. I wish I did 4. No, I haven't. I wish I had 5. No, they
aren't. I wish they were 6. No, he doesn't. I wish he did 7. No,
they aren't. I wish they were 8. No, it isn't. I wish it was 9. No, I
can't. I wish I could 10. No, I haven't. I wish I had

(b) 1. Yes, they are. I wish they weren't 2. Yes, he does. I wish he
didn't 3. Yes, I must. I wish I didn't have to 4. Yes, they are. I wish
they weren't 5. Yes, they do. I wish they didn't 6. Yes, I have. I
wish I hadn't 7. Yes, he is. I wish he wasn't 8. Yes, I must. I wish I
didn't have to 9. Yes, I have. I wish I hadn't 10. Yes, I must. I wish
I didn't have to

Drill 93 Each answer begins *I wish . . . (Was* is replaceable by *were.*)
1. I had a flat here 2. I knew five languages 3. I lived near my
work 4. I could park outside my office 5. my case was quite
light 6. I was getting thinner 7. I had six weeks' holiday a year
8. my son wrote every week 9. my boss handed out free theatre
tickets 10. I'd worked hard all the year 11. I got the weekends
off 12. I had plenty of time for reading 13. my neighbours were very
quiet 14. I got a bonus at Christmas 15. I found it easy to
concentrate 16. I understood it 17. I could take a day off any
time 18. I'd saved £100 19. my house looked out on a park 20. my
parents gave me an allowance
If only answers are exactly the same but require a more dramatic tone
of voice.

Drill 94 (a) Each answer has the form *I wish you'd . . . Tom too.* or:
If only you'd . . .
1. paid 2. invited 3. scolded 4. stopped 5. rung 6. written
to 7. voted for 8. suggested 9. spoken to 10. warned

(b) Each answer begins *I wish you hadn't . . .* or: *If only you
hadn't . . .*
1. said anything 2. eaten anything 3. drunk anything 4. tipped
anyone 5. given anything 6. signed anything 7. photographed
anything 8. admitted anything 9. taken anything 10. told anyone

Drill 95 (a) Put *would you* before the request you are asked to make,
and add *please* e.g. *Would you tell Jack, please?* (b) As above, but use
Could you.

Drill 96 (a) Put: *If you'd* before the request you are asked to make.
e.g. *If you'd open your case.* (b) Put: *Would you like to . . .* before the
request you are asked to make. e.g. *Would you like to open your case*

Drill 97 (a) Each answer begins *No. Would you mind . . .* (b) Each answer begins: *No. I wonder if you'd mind . . .* Otherwise (a) and (b) answers are identical.
1. making them 2. laying it 3. sweeping them 4. grinding it
5. cutting them up 6. doing it 7. paying it 8. scrubbing them
9. polishing it 10. dusting it 11. doing it 12. ironing them
13. making it 14. collecting it 15. winding it 16. grating it
17. posting them 18. cutting them 19. peeling them 20. frying them

Drill 98 (a) Each answer has the form *Would you mind if I . . . tomorrow instead?* (b) Each answer has the form *Would it be all right if I . . . tomorrow instead?* Otherwise (a) and (b) answers are identical.
1. left 2. rang them 3. told him 4. paid it 5. wrote to her
6. sent it 7. bought them 8. began 9. reported it 10. mended it 11. made it 12. changed it 13. checked them 14. renewed it 15. did it 16. booked them 17. decided 18. moved out
19. made it 20. settled it

Drill 99 (a) Each answer begins *I'd rather . . .* (b) Each answer begins *I'd prefer to . . .* Otherwise (a) and (b) answers are identical.
1. go out to supper 2. join an eleven o'clock class 3. fly 4. pay by cheque 5. marry a rich man 6. go out to work 7. ring him
8. cook it 9. watch tennis 10. see a play 11. borrow one
12. leave tomorrow 13. ask Jack 14. spend it 15. read the book first 16. take them to the launderette 17. look for a taxi
18. explain it in English 19. be driven 20. live nearer the ground

Drill 100 (a) Each answer begins *I'd rather you . . .*
1. bought a small dog 2. wrote to me 3. studied mathematics
4. turned it with a knife 5. put it in the bank 6. hung it on the line 7. spoke English 8. paid cash 9. settled it today 10. climbed with a guide 11. left it under the mat 12. asked the garage to do it 13. stayed at home 14. said nothing 15. answered it
16. turned it off 17. wore a suit 18. went to a hairdresser
19. drove slowly 20. registered it

(b) Replace *I'd rather you* + past tense by *I'd prefer you* + infinitive. The rest of each answer is the same as the (a) answer. Note that the full infinitive is necessary. e.g. *I'd prefer you to buy . . .*